WILEY CPA
EXAM REVIEW

FOCUS NOTES

OCT -- 2013

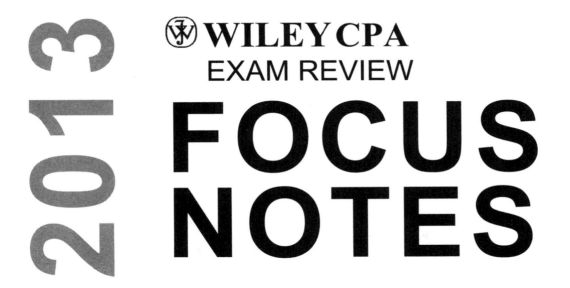

2013

WILEY CPA
EXAM REVIEW

FOCUS NOTES

Financial Accounting and Reporting

CONTENTS

Preface	*vii*
About the Author	*ix*
Basic Concepts	1
Financial Statements	8
Inventories	36
Long-Term Construction Contracts	57
Fixed Assets	61
Monetary Assets & Liabilities	87
Leases	116
Bonds	130
Debt Restructure	142
Pensions	146
Deferred Taxes	152
Stockholders' Equity	161
Investments	187
Statement of Cash Flows	198

Consolidated Statements   207

Derivative Instruments   221

Segment Reporting   232

    Partnership   235

    Foreign Currency   243

    Interim Reporting   247

    Personal Financial Statements   251

Governmental (State and Local) Accounting   254

Not-For-Profit Accounting   301

Index   314

PREFACE

This publication is a comprehensive, yet simplified study program. It provides a review of all the basic skills and concepts tested on the CPA exam, and teaches important strategies to take the exam faster and more accurately. This tool allows you to take control of the CPA exam.

This simplified and focused approach to studying for the CPA exam can be used:

- As a handy and convenient reference manual
- To solve exam questions
- To reinforce material being studied

Included is all of the information necessary to obtain a passing score on the CPA exam in a concise and easy-to-use format. Due to the wide variety of information covered on the exam, a number of techniques are included:

- Acronyms and mnemonics to help candidates learn and remember a variety of rules and checklists
- Formulas and equations that simplify complex calculations required on the exam
- Simplified outlines of key concepts without the details that encumber or distract from learning the essential elements
- Techniques that can be applied to problem solving or essay writing, such as preparing a multiple-step income statement, determining who will prevail in a legal conflict, or developing an audit program

- Pro forma statements, reports, and schedules that make it easy to prepare these items by simply filling in the blanks
- Proven techniques to help you become a smarter, sharper, and more accurate test taker

This publication may also be useful to university students enrolled in Intermediate, Advanced and Cost Accounting; Auditing, Business Law, and Federal Income Tax classes; Economics, and Finance classes.

Good Luck on the Exam,

Ray Whittington, PhD, CPA

ABOUT THE AUTHOR

Ray Whittington, PhD, CPA, CMA, CIA, is the dean of the College of Commerce at DePaul University. Prior to joining the faculty at DePaul, Professor Whittington was the Director of Accountancy at San Diego State University. From 1989 through 1991, he was the Director of Auditing Research for the American Institute of Certified Public Accountants (AICPA), and he previously was on the audit staff of KPMG. He previously served as a member of the Auditing Standards Board of the AICPA and as a member of the Accounting and Review Services Committee and the Board of Regents of the Institute of Internal Auditors. Professor Whittington has published numerous textbooks, articles, monographs, and continuing education courses.

ABOUT THE CONTRIBUTOR

Natalie T. Churyk, PhD, CPA is the Caterpillar Professor of Accountancy at Northern Illinois University. She teaches in the undergraduate and M.A.S. programs as well as developing and delivering continuing professional education in Northern Illinois University's CPA and CIA Review programs. Professor Churyk has published in professional and academic journals. She serves on state and national committees relating to education and student initiatives and is a member of several editorial review boards. Professor Churyk is a coauthor on two textbooks: *Accounting and Auditing Research: Tools and Strategies* and *Mastering the Codification and eIFRS: A Case Approach.*

OBJECTIVES OF FINANCIAL REPORTING

Financial statements are designed to meet the objectives of financial reporting:

Balance Sheet	Direct Information	Financial Position
Statement of Earnings and Comprehensive Income	Direct Information	Entity Performance
Statement of Cash Flows	Direct Information	Entity Cash Flows
Financial Statements Taken As a Whole	Indirect Information	Management & Performance

Qualitative Characteristics of Accounting Information

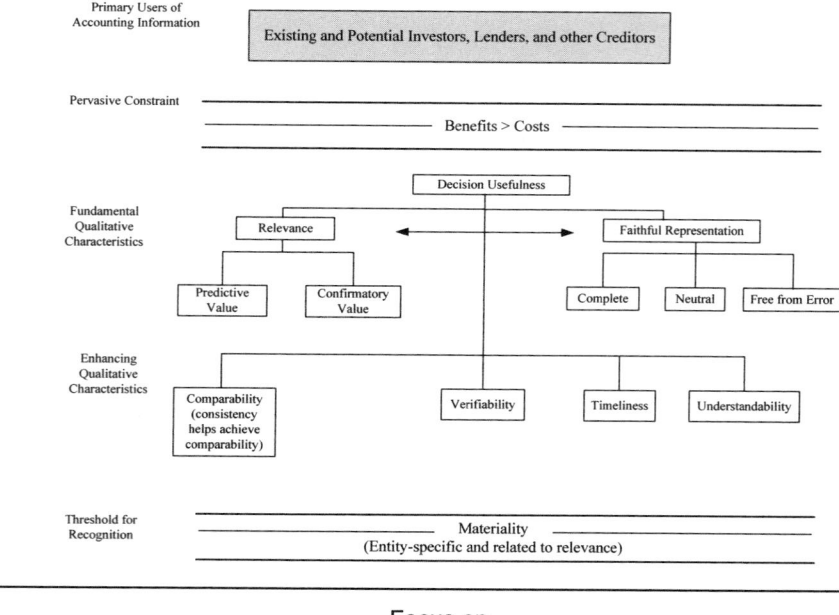

Primary Users of Accounting Information

Existing and Potential Investors, Lenders, and other Creditors

Pervasive Constraint

Benefits > Costs

Decision Usefulness

Fundamental Qualitative Characteristics

Relevance

Faithful Representation

Predictive Value

Confirmatory Value

Complete

Neutral

Free from Error

Enhancing Qualitative Characteristics

Comparability (consistency helps achieve comparability)

Verifiability

Timeliness

Understandability

Threshold for Recognition

Materiality
(Entity-specific and related to relevance)

Focus on
Basic Concepts – Module 9

2

IFRS® and US Conceptual Framework as converged

**Fundamental characteristics/
Decision usefulness**

Relevance

Predictive value

Feedback value

Materiality

Faithful representation

Completeness

Neutrality

Free from error

Enhancing characteristics

Comparability

Verifiability

Timeliness

Understandability

Constraints

Benefit vs. costs

Elements of Financial Statements

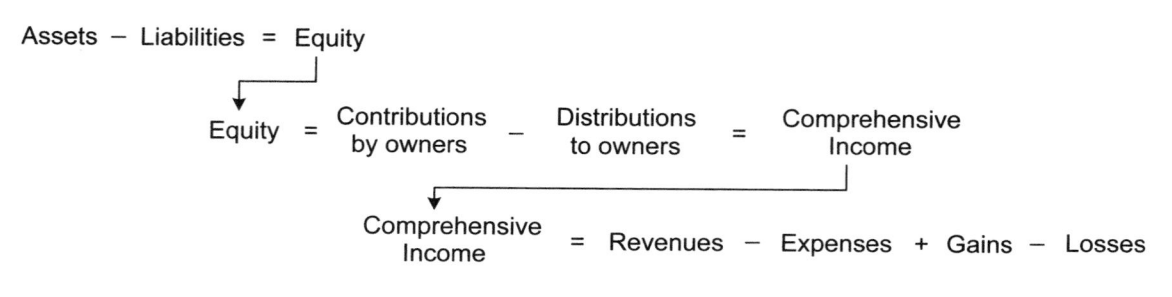

Assets − Liabilities = Equity

Equity = Contributions by owners − Distributions to owners = Comprehensive Income

Comprehensive Income = Revenues − Expenses + Gains − Losses

Comprehensive Income = Net income ± Adjustments to stockholders' equity

IFRS Elements

Assets

Liabilities

Equity

Income (includes both revenues and gains)

Expense (includes expenses and losses)

BASIC RULES & CONCEPTS

Consistency

Realization

Recognition

Allocation

Matching

Full disclosure

Revenue Recognition

Accrual method	Collection reasonably assured
	Degree of uncollectibility estimable
Installment sale	Collection not reasonably assured
Cost recovery	Collection not reasonably assured
	No basis for determining whether or not collectible

Installment Sales Method

Installment receivable balance

× Gross profit percentage

= Deferred gross profit (balance sheet)

Cash collections

× Gross profit percentage

= Realized gross profit (income statement)

Cost Recovery Method

All collections applied to cost before any profit or interest income is recognized

Converting from Cash Basis to Accrual Basis

Revenues

Cash (amount received)	xx	
Increase in accounts receivable (given)	xx	
Decrease in accounts receivable (given)		xx
Revenues (plug)		xx

Cost of Sales

Cost of sales (plug)	xx	
Increase in inventory (given)	xx	
Decrease in accounts payable (given)	xx	
Decrease in inventory (given)		xx
Increase in accounts payable (given)		xx
Cash (payments for merchandise)		xx

Expenses

Expense (plug)	xx	
Increase in prepaid expenses (given)	xx	
Decrease in accrued expenses (given)	xx	
Decrease in prepaid expenses (given)		xx
Increase in accrued expenses (given)		xx
Cash (amount paid for expense)		xx

Balance Sheet

Current Assets
- Cash
- Trading securities
- Current securities available for sale
- Accounts receivable
- Inventories
- Prepaid expenses
- Current deferred tax asset

Current Liabilities
- Short-term debt
- Accounts payable
- Accrued expenses
- Current income taxes payable
- Current deferred tax liability
- Current portion of long-term debt
- Unearned revenues

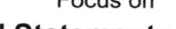

Balance Sheet (continued)

Long-Term Investments
Noncurrent securities available for sale
Securities held to maturity
Investments at cost or equity

Property, Plant, & Equipment

Intangibles

Other Assets
Deposits
Deferred charges
Noncurrent deferred tax asset

Long-Term Debt
Long-term notes payable
Bonds payable
Noncurrent deferred tax liability

Stockholders' Equity
Preferred stock
Common stock
Additional paid-in capital
Retained earnings
Accumulated other comprehensive income

Current Assets & Liabilities

Assets
- Economic resource
- Future benefit
- Control of company
- Past event or transaction

Liabilities
- Economic obligation
- Future sacrifice
- Beyond control of company
- Past event or transaction

Current Assets
- Converted into cash or used up

Longer of:
One year
One accounting cycle

Current Liabilities
- Paid or settled
- OR Requires use of current assets

Longer of:
One year
One accounting cycle

IFRS and Current Liabilities

- Short-term obligations expected to be refinanced must be classified as current liabilities unless there is an agreement in place prior to the balance sheet date.
- A "provision" is a liability that is uncertain in timing or amount
  - If outcome is probable and measurable, it is not considered a contingency
  - Probable means greater than 50%
- A "contingency is not recognized because it is not probable that an outflow will be required or the amount cannot be measured reliably
  - Contingencies are disclosed unless probability is remote

Special Disclosures

Significant Accounting Policies

Inventory method

Depreciation method

Criteria for classifying investments

Method of accounting for long-term construction contracts

Subsequent Events

An event occurring after the balance sheet date but before the financial statements are issued or available to be issued. Measured through the issuance date.

Two types of events are possible:

1. Events that provide additional evidence about conditions existing at the balance sheet date (recognize in the financial statements)
2. Events that provide evidence about conditions that did not exist at the balance sheet date but arise subsequent to that date (disclose in the notes)

IFRS: Subsequent events measured through the date the financial statements are authorized to be issued.

Related-Party Transactions

Exceptions:

Salary
Expense reimbursements
Ordinary transactions

Reporting the Results of Operations

Preparing an Income Statement

Multiple step		Single step	
Revenues		Revenues	
−	Cost of sales	+	Other income
=	Gross profit	+	Gains
−	Operating expenses	=	Total revenues
	Selling expenses	−	Costs and expenses
	G & A expenses		Cost of sales
=	Operating income		Selling expenses
+	Other income		G & A expenses
+	Gains		Other expenses
−	Other expenses		Losses
−	Losses		Income tax expense
=	Income before taxes	=	Income from continuing operations
−	Income tax expense		
=	Income from continuing operations		

Computing Net Income

Income from continuing operations (either approach)

± **D**iscontinued operations

± **E**xtraordinary items

= Net income

(Cumulative changes section was eliminated by precodification SFAS 154)

IFRS Income Statement

- Revenue (referred to as income)
- Finance costs (interest expense)
- Share of profits and losses of associates and joint ventures accounted for using equity method
- Tax expense
- Discontinued operations
- Profit or loss
- Noncontrolling interest in profit and loss
- Net profit (loss) attributable to equity holders in the parent
- No extraordinary items under IFRS

Errors Affecting Income

Error (ending balance)

	Current stmt	Prior stmt
Asset overstated	Overstated	No effect
Asset understated	Understated	No effect
Liability overstated	Understated	No effect
Liability understated	Overstated	No effect

Error (beginning balance – ending balance is correct)

Asset overstated	Understated	Overstated
Asset understated	Overstated	Understated
Liability overstated	Overstated	Understated
Liability understated	Understated	Overstated

Errors Affecting Income (continued)

Error (beginning balance – ending balance is not correct)

Asset overstated	No effect	Overstated
Asset understated	No effect	Understated
Liability overstated	No effect	Understated
Liability understated	No effect	Overstated

Extraordinary Items

Classification as extraordinary – 2 requirements (both must apply)

- Unusual in nature
- Infrequent of occurrence

One or neither applies – component of income from continuing operations

Extraordinary

A hail storm damages all of a farmer's crops in a location where hail storms have never occurred

Acts of nature (usually)

Not Extraordinary

Gains or losses on sales of investments or property, plant, & equipment

Gains or losses due to changes in foreign currency exchange rates

Write-offs of inventory or receivables

Effects of major strikes or changes in value of investments

Change in Accounting Principle: Allowed only if required by new accounting principles or change to preferable method

Use retrospective application of new principle:

1) Calculate revised balance of asset or liability as of beginning of period as if new principle had always been in use.
2) Compare balance to amount reported under old method.
3) Multiply difference by 100% minus tax rate.
4) Result is treated on books as prior period adjustment to beginning retained earnings.

   a) Note: Indirect effects (e.g., changes in bonus plans) are reported only in period of change.

5) All previous periods being presented in comparative statements restated to new principle.
6) Beginning balance of earliest presented statement of retained earnings adjusted for all effects going back before that date.
7) IFRS: Similar rules—Voluntary change must provide more reliable and relevant information.

Change in Accounting Principle (continued)

Journal entry:

Asset or liability	xxx	
Retained earnings		xxx
Current or deferred tax liability (asset)		xxx

Or

Retained earnings	xxx	
Current or deferred tax liability (asset)	xxx	
Asset or liability		xxx

Special Changes

Changes in accounting principle are handled using the **prospective** method under limited circumstances. No calculation is made of prior period effects and the new principle is simply applied starting at the beginning of the current year when the following changes in principle occur:

- Changes in the method of depreciation, amortization, or depletion
- Changes whose effect on prior periods is impractical to determine (e.g. changes to LIFO when records don't allow computation of earlier LIFO cost bases)

(Note: the method of handling changes in accounting principle described here under ASC 250-10 replaces earlier approaches, which applied the **cumulative method** to most changes in accounting principle. Precodification SFAS 154 abolished the use of the cumulative method.)

Change in Estimate

- No retrospective application
- Change applied as of beginning of current period
- Applied in current and future periods

Error Corrections

Applies to:

- Change from unacceptable principle to acceptable principle
- Errors in prior period financial statements

When error occurred:

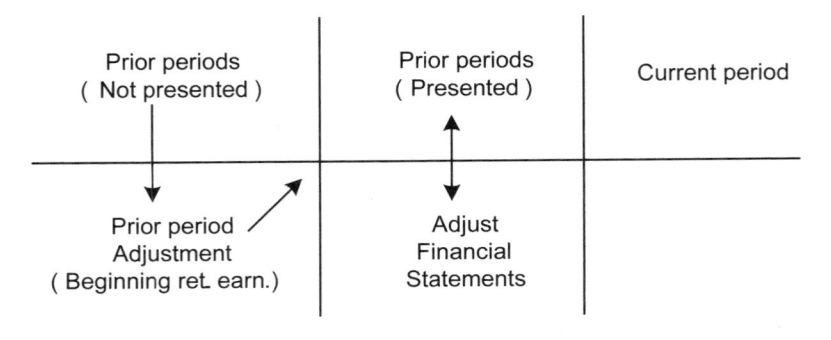

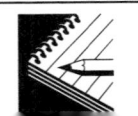

Discontinued Operations

When components of a business are disposed of, their results are reported in discontinued operations:

- Component – An asset group whose activities can be distinguished from the remainder of the entity both operationally and for financial reporting purposes.
- Disposal – Either the assets have already been disposed of or they are being held for sale and the entity is actively searching for a buyer and believes a sale is probable at a price that can be reasonably estimated.

All activities related to the component are reported in discontinued operations, including those occurring prior to the commitment to dispose and in prior periods being presented for comparative purposes.

Reporting Discontinued Operations

Lower section of the income statement:

- After income from continuing operations
- Before extraordinary items

Reported amount each year includes all activities related to the component from operations as well as gains and losses on disposal, net of income tax effects

- Expected gains and losses from operations in future periods are not reported until the future period in which they occur.

Impairment loss is included in the current period when the fair market value of the component is believed to be lower than carrying amount based on the anticipated sales price of the component in future period.

Reporting Comprehensive Income

Statement of Comprehensive Income required as one of financial statements

- May be part of Income statement
- May be separate statement
- Begin with net income
- Add or subtract items of other comprehensive income

Other comprehensive income includes:

- Current year's unrealized gains or losses on securities available for sale
- Current year's foreign currency translation adjustments
- Current year's unrealized gains or losses resulting from changes in market values of certain derivatives being used as cash flow hedges

Accounting for Changing Prices

Accounting at Current Cost

Assets & liabilities reported at current amounts

Income statement items adjusted to current amounts

- Inventory reported at replacement cost
- Cost of sales = Number of units sold × Average current cost of units during period
- Differences in inventory & cost of sales treated as holding gains or losses
- Depreciation & amortization – Computed using same method & life based on current cost

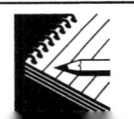

Accounting for Changes in Price Level

Purchasing power gains & losses relate only to **monetary** items

- Monetary assets – money or claim to receive money such as cash & net receivables
- Monetary liabilities – obligations to pay specific amounts of money

Company may be monetary creditor or debtor

- Monetary creditor – monetary assets > monetary liabilities
- Monetary debtor – monetary liabilities > monetary assets

In periods of rising prices

- Monetary creditor will experience purchasing power loss
- Monetary debtor will experience purchasing power gain

SEC Reporting Requirements

Regulation S-X describes form and content to be filed

Regulation S-K describes information requirements

- Form S-1 (US)/F-1 (foreign)—registration statement
- Form 8-K (US)/6-K (foreign)—material event
- Form 10-K (US)/20F (foreign)—annual report
- Form 10Q—quarterly report
- Schedule 14A—proxy statement

Regulation AB—describes asset-backed securities reporting

Regulation Fair Disclosure (FD)—mandates material information disclosures

Fair Value Measurements

Six-step application process

1. Identify asset or liability to measure
2. Determine principle or advantageous market
3. Determine valuation premise
4. Determine valuation technique
5. Obtain inputs (levels)
6. Calculate fair value

Multiple disclosures for assets/liabilities measured at fair value on a recurring/nonrecurring basis

Fair Value Concepts

Fair value—the price that would be received to sell an asset or paid to transfer a liability in an orderly transaction between market participants at the measurement date (exit price) under current market conditions

Principal market (greatest volume of activity)

Most advantageous market (maximizes price received or minimizes amount paid)

Highest and best use—maximize the value of the asset or group of assets

Valuation techniques

    Market approach—uses prices and relevant market transaction information

    Income approach—converts future amounts to a single current (discounted) amount

    Cost approach—current replacement cost

Fair Value Concepts (continued)

Fair value hierarchy (level 1, 2, and 3 inputs)

    Level 1—quoted market prices

    Level 2—directly or indirectly observable inputs other than quoted market prices

    Level 3—unobservable inputs

Fair value option—an election to value certain financial assets and financial liabilities at fair value

INVENTORIES

Goods In Transit

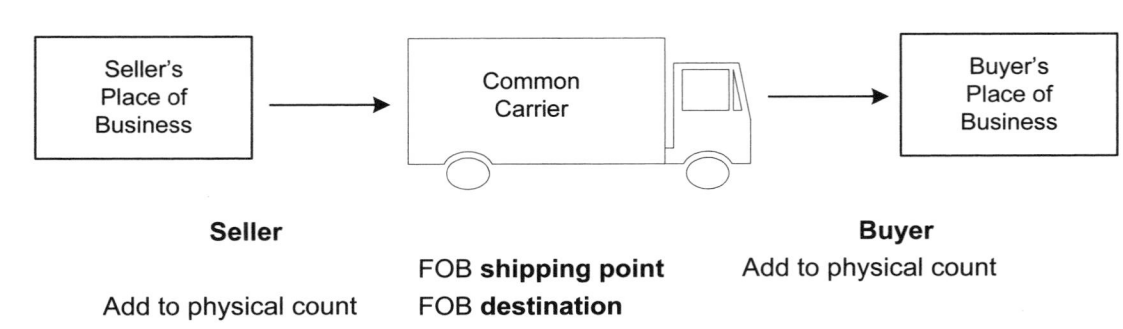

| Seller's Place of Business | → | Common Carrier | → | Buyer's Place of Business |

Seller

Add to physical count

FOB **shipping point**
FOB **destination**

Buyer

Add to physical count

Goods In Transit (continued)

Inventory Cost

Purchase price
+ Freight in
+ Costs incurred in preparing for sale
= Inventory cost

Goods on Consignment

Consignee — Exclude from physical count
Consignor — Add to physical count (at cost)

Cost of goods on consignment =
Inventory cost
+ Cost of shipping to consignee

Abnormal costs expensed in current period instead of being included in inventory:

- Idle facility expense
- Wasted materials in production
- Double freight when items returned and redelivered

Cost of Goods Sold

Beginning inventory

+   Net purchases

=   Cost of goods available for sale

–   Ending inventory

=   Cost of goods sold

Inventory Errors

	Beg. RE	COGS	Gross Profit	End RE
Beginning – overstated	Over	Over	Under	No effect
Beginning – understated	Under	Under	Over	No effect
Ending – overstated	No effect	Under	Over	Over
Ending – understated	No effect	Over	Under	Under

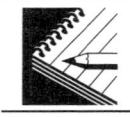

Periodic Versus Perpetual

	Periodic	**Perpetual**
Buy merchandise:	Purchases	Inventory
	Accounts payable	Accounts payable
Sell merchandise	Accounts receivable	Accounts receivable
	Sales	Sales
		Cost of goods sold
		Inventory
Record cost of goods sold	Ending inventory (count)	
	Cost of goods sold (plug)	
	Purchases (net amount)	
	Beginning inventory (balance)	

FIFO – Same under either method

LIFO – Different amounts for periodic and perpetual

Average – Different amounts for periodic and perpetual

      Periodic – Weighted-average

Inventory Valuation Methods

	Ending Inventory	Cost of Goods Sold	Gross Profit
Periods of rising prices:			
FIFO	Highest	Lowest	Highest
LIFO	Lowest	Highest	Lowest
Periods of falling prices:			
FIFO	Lowest	Highest	Lowest
LIFO	Highest	Lowest	Highest

Applying LIFO

Step 1 – Determine ending quantity

Step 2 – Compare to previous period's ending quantity

Step 3 – Increases – Add new layer

Step 4 – Small decreases (less than most recent layer) – Reduce most recent layer

Step 5 – Large decreases (more than most recent layer) – Eliminate most recent layer or layers and decrease next most recent layer

Step 6 – Apply appropriate unit price to each layer

For each layer:

Inventory quantity   ×   Price per unit   =   Inventory value

Application of LIFO

Information given:

	Ending Quantity	Price per unit
Year 1	10,000 units	$5.00
Year 2	12,000 units	$5.50
Year 3	15,000 units	$6.00
Year 4	13,500 units	$6.50
Year 5	11,200 units	$7.00
Year 6	13,200 units	$7.50

Information applied:

Year 1:

Base layer	10,000 units	$5.00	$50,000
Total	**10,000 units**		**$50,000**

Application of LIFO (continued)

Year 2:

Year 2 layer	2,000 units	$5.50	$11,000
Base layer	10,000 units	$5.00	$50,000
Total	**12,000 units**		**$61,000**

Year 3:

Year 3 layer	3,000 units	$6.00	$18,000
Year 2 layer	2,000 units	$5.50	$11,000
Base layer	10,000 units	$5.00	$50,000
Total	**15,000 units**		**$79,000**

Application of LIFO (continued)

Year 4:

	Units	Price	Amount
Year 3 layer	1,500 units	$6.00	$9,000
Year 2 layer	2,000 units	$5.50	$11,000
Base layer	10,000 units	$5.00	$50,000
Total	**13,500 units**		**$70,000**

Year 5:

	Units	Price	Amount
Year 2 layer	1,200 units	$5.50	$6,600
Base layer	10,000 units	$5.00	$50,000
Total	**11,200 units**		**$56,600**

Application of LIFO (continued)

Year 6:

Year 3 layer	2,000 units	$7.50	$15,000
Year 2 layer	1,200 units	$5.50	$6,600
Base layer	10,000 units	$5.00	$50,000
Total	**13,200 units**		**$71,600**

Dollar-Value LIFO

Less cumbersome than LIFO for inventory consisting of many items

Combines inventory into pools

Increases in some items within a pool offset decreases in others

Applying Dollar-Value LIFO

Step 1 – Determine ending inventory at current year's prices

Step 2 – Divide by current price level index to convert to base year prices

Step 3 – Compare to previous period's ending inventory at base year prices

Step 4 – Increases – Add new layer at base year prices

Step 5 – Small decreases (less than most recent layer) – Reduce most recent layer

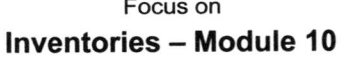

Applying Dollar-Value LIFO (continued)

Step 6 – Large decreases (more than most recent layer) – Eliminate most recent layer or layers and decrease next most recent layer

Step 7 – Apply appropriate unit price to each layer

For each layer:

Inventory amount at base   ×   Price   =   Inventory amount
year prices   index   Dollar-Value LIFO

Application of Dollar-Value LIFO

Information given:

	Ending Inventory at Current Prices	Price level index
Year 1	$200,000	100
Year 2	243,800	106
Year 3	275,000	110
Year 4	255,200	116

Information applied:

Year 1

		Base year prices	Index	Dollar-Value LIFO
Base layer		$200,000	100	$200,000
	Total	$200,000		$200,000

Application of Dollar-Value LIFO (continued)

Year 2:

$243,800 ÷ 1.06 = $230,000 (at base year prices)

	Base year prices	Index	Dollar-Value LIFO
Year 2 layer	$30,000	106	$31,800
Base layer	$200,000	100	$200,000
Total	$230,000		$231,800

Application of Dollar-Value LIFO (continued)

Year 3:

$275,000 ÷ 1.10 = $250,000 (at base year prices)

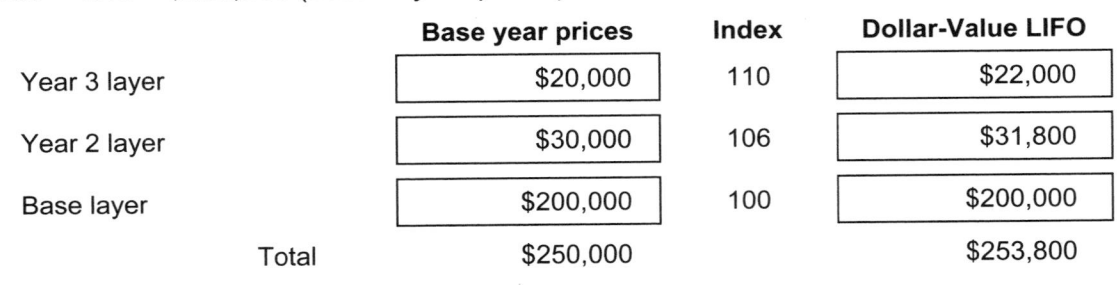

	Base year prices	Index	Dollar-Value LIFO
Year 3 layer	$20,000	110	$22,000
Year 2 layer	$30,000	106	$31,800
Base layer	$200,000	100	$200,000
Total	$250,000		$253,800

Application of Dollar-Value LIFO (continued)

Year 4:

$255,200 \div 1.16 = \$220,000$ (at base year prices)

	Base year prices	Index	Dollar-Value LIFO
Year 2 layer	$20,000	106	$21,200
Base layer	$200,000	100	$200,000
Total	$220,000		$221,200

Dollar-Value LIFO – Calculating a Price Level Index

Simplified LIFO – Company uses a published index

Double Extension Method – Cumulative index

Compare current year to base year

$$\frac{\text{Ending inventory at current year's prices}}{\text{Ending inventory at base year prices}}$$

Link Chain Method – Annual index

Compare current year to previous year

$$\frac{\text{Ending inventory at current year's prices}}{\text{Ending inventory at previous year's prices}}$$

Lower of Cost or Market

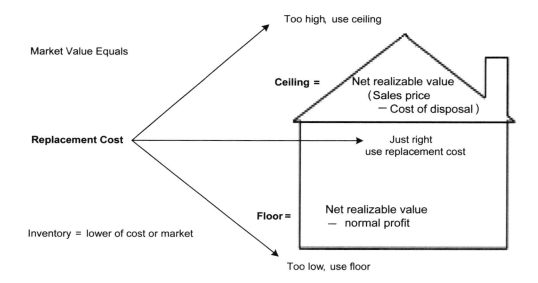

Market Value Equals

Too high, use ceiling

Ceiling = Net realizable value
(Sales price
— Cost of disposal)

Replacement Cost

Just right
use replacement cost

Floor = Net realizable value
— normal profit

Inventory = lower of cost or market

Too low, use floor

Gross Profit Method for Estimating Inventory

If gross profit is **percentage of sales:**

	Sales	100%
−	Cost of sales	
=	Gross profit	

If gross profit is **percentage of cost:**

	Sales	
−	Cost of sales	100%
=	Gross profit	

To find cost of sales

Sales × (100% − Gross profit %)

Sales ÷ (100% + Gross profit%)

	Beginning inventory
+	Net purchases
=	Cost of goods available
−	Cost of sales
=	Ending inventory

Conventional Retail (Lower of Cost or Market)

	Cost	Retail	C/R%
Beginning inventory	xx	xx	
+ Net purchases	xx	xx	
+ Freight in	xx		
+ Net markups		xx	
= Cost of goods available for sale	xx	xx	Cost / Retail
− Sales (retail)	xx		
Net markdowns	xx		
Employee discounts	xx		
Spoilage (retail)	xx	(xx)	
= Ending inventory at retail		xx	
× Cost to retail percentage		x%	
= Ending inventory at approximate lower of cost or market		xx	

IFRS: Inventory

- LIFO Not permissible
- Lower of cost or net realizable value (LCNRV) on item-by-item basis
- Biological assets carried at fair value less costs to sell at the point of harvest.

LONG-TERM CONSTRUCTION CONTRACTS

Percentage of Completion

Use when:

- Estimates of costs are reasonably dependable
- Estimates of progress toward completion

Reporting profit

- Recognized proportionately during contract
- Added to construction in process

Balance sheet amount

- Current asset – excess of costs and estimated profits over billings
- Current liability – excess of billings over costs and estimated profits

Calculating profit

Step 1 – Total profit

Contract price		xxx
Total estimated cost		
Cost incurred to date (**1**)	xxx	
Estimated cost to complete	+ <u>xxx</u>	
Total estimated cost (**2**)		– <u>xxx</u>
Total estimated profit (**3**)		= <u>xxx</u>

Step 2 – % of completion (Cost to cost method)

Costs incurred to date (**1**) ÷ Total estimated cost (**2**) = % of completion (**4**)

Step 3 – Profit to date

% of completion (**4**) × Total estimated profit (**3**) = Estimated profit to date (**5**)

Step 4 – Current period's profit

Estimated profit to date (**5**) – Profit previously recognized = Current period's profit

Recognizing Losses

When loss expected:

Estimated loss	xxx
+ Profit recognized to date	xxx
= Amount of loss to recognize	xxx

Completed Contract

Income statement amount

- Profit recognized in period of completion
- Loss recognized in earliest period estimable

Balance sheet amount

- Current assets – excess of costs over billings
- Current liabilities – excess of billings over costs

IFRS Construction Contracts

- Prohibits completed contract method

PROPERTY, PLANT, & EQUIPMENT

General Rule

Capitalized amount = Cost of asset + Costs incurred in preparing it for its intended use

    Cost of asset = FMV of asset received **or**

        Cash paid + FMV of assets given

Gifts:

Asset (FMV)	xx	
Income		xx

Other capitalized costs for assets acquired by gift or purchase:

Shipping
Insurance during shipping
Installation
Testing

Land and Building

Total cost:

> Purchase price
> Delinquent taxes assumed
> Legal fees
> Title insurance

Allocation to land and building – **Relative Fair Market Value Method**

> FMV of land
> +   <u>FMV of building</u>
> =   Total FMV

Land = FMV of land ÷ Total FMV × Total Cost

Building = FMV of building ÷ Total FMV × Total Cost

Capitalization of Interest

Capitalize on:

    Assets constructed for company's use

    Assets manufactured for resale resulting from special order

Do not capitalize on:

    Inventory manufactured in the ordinary course of business

Interest capitalized:

    Interest on debt incurred for construction of asset

Interest on other debt that could be avoided by repayment of debt

Computed on:

    Weighted-average accumulated expenditures

Costs Incurred After Acquisition

Capitalize if:

- **Bigger** – the cost makes the asset bigger, such as an addition to a building
- **Better** – the cost makes the asset better, such as an improvement that makes an asset perform more efficiently
- **Longer** – the cost makes the asset last longer, it extends the useful life

Do not capitalize:

Repairs and maintenance

Depreciation and Depletion

Basic Terms:

Straight-line rate = 100% ÷ Useful life (in years)

Book value = Cost − Accumulated depreciation

Depreciable basis = Cost − Salvage value

Selection of Method:

Use **straight-line** when benefit from asset is uniform over life

Use **accelerated** when:

- Asset more productive in earlier years
- Costs of maintenance increase in later years
- Risk of obsolescence is high

Use **units-of-production** when usefulness decreases with use

Straight-Line	Double-Declining Balance
Annual depreciation =	Annual depreciation =
Depreciable basis	**Book value**
× Straight-line rate	× Straight-line rate
	× 2
Partial year =	Partial year =
Annual depreciation	Book value
× Portion of year	× Straight-line rate
	× 2
	× Portion of year

Sum-of-the-Years' Digits

Annual depreciation = **Depreciable basis** × Fraction

	1st Year	**2nd Year**	**3rd Year**
Numerator =	n	n–1	n–2
Denominator =	n(n+1) ÷ 2	n(n+1) ÷ 2	n(n+1) ÷ 2

Partial year:

1st year =	1st year's depreciation × portion of year
2nd year =	Remainder of 1st year's depreciation
	+ 2nd year's depreciation × portion of year
3rd year =	Remainder of 2nd year's depreciation
	+ 3rd year's depreciation × portion of year

Units-of-Production

Depreciation rate = **Depreciable basis** ÷ Total estimated units to be produced (hours)

Annual depreciation = Depreciation rate × Number of units produced (hours used)

Group or Composite

Based on straight-line

Gains or losses not recognized on disposal

Cash (proceeds)	xx	
Accumulated depreciation (plug)	xx	
Asset (original cost)		xx

Impairment

Occurs if undiscounted future cash flow less than asset carrying amount from events such as:

- A decrease in the market value of the asset
- An adverse action or assessment by a regulator
- An operating or cash flow loss associated with a revenue producing asset

When an impairment loss occurs:

- Asset is written down to fair market value (or discounted net cash flow):

Loss due to impairment	xx	
Accumulated depreciation		xx

Note that test for impairment (future cash flow) is different from write-down amount (net realizable value).

Application of Impairment Rules

Example 1:

    Asset carrying value – $1,000,000

    Undiscounted future cash flow expected from asset – $900,000

    Fair market value of asset – $600,000

    Impairment exists – $900,000 expected cash flow less than $1,000,000 carrying amount

    Write asset down by $400,000 ($1,000,000 reduced to $600,000)

Example 2:

    Asset carrying value – $800,000

    Undiscounted future cash flow expected from asset – $900,000

    Fair market value of asset – $600,000

    No impairment adjustment – $900,000 expected cash flow exceeds $800,000 carrying amount

Disposal of Property, Plant, & Equipment

Cash (proceeds)	xx	
Accumulated depreciation (balance)	xx	
Loss on disposal (plug)	xx	
Gain on disposal (plug)		xx
Asset (original cost)		xx

A disposal in **involuntary conversion** is recorded in the same manner as a sale.

IFRS Impairment

- Focuses on events (e.g., breach of contract or significant financial difficulty of the issuer)
- Loss recorded income
- IFRS: Reversal of losses on investments in debt allowed

Nonmonetary Exchanges

Cash (amount received)		
Asset – New (FMV)	xx	
Accumulated depreciation (balance on old asset)	xx	
Loss on disposal (plug)		
Cash (amount paid)		
Gain on disposal (plug)		xx
Asset – Old (Original cost)		xx

FMV

Use fair value of asset received **or**

Fair value of asset given

\+   Cash paid

–   Cash received

Nonmonetary Exchanges (continued)

Exception

Applies to exchanges when:

- FMV is not determinable
- Exchange is only to facilitate subsequent sales to customers (e.g. ownership of inventory in one city is swapped for similar inventory in another to facilitate prompt delivery to customer in distant city)
- Transaction lacks commercial substance (risk, timing, and amount of future cash flows will not significantly change as a result of the transaction)

Loss – FMV of asset given < Carrying value of asset given

Cash (amount received)	xx	
Asset – New (FMV)	xx	
Loss on disposal (plug)	xx	
Cash (amount paid)		xx
Asset – Old (carrying value)		xx

Nonmonetary Exchanges (continued)

Gain – FMV of asset given > Carrying value of asset given

Gain recognized only when cash received

FMV of asset given
  − Carrying value of asset given
  = Total gain
  × Percentage
  = Gain recognized

$$\frac{\text{Cash received}}{\text{Total proceeds (Cash + FMV of asset received)}}$$

Cash (amount received)	xx	
Asset—New (plug)	xx	
Gain on disposal (computed amount)		xx
Asset—Old (carrying value)		xx

Nonmonetary Exchanges (continued)

No gain recognized when cash paid or no cash involved

Asset – New (plug)	xx	
Accumulated depreciation (balance on old asset)	xx	
Cash (amount paid)		xx
Asset – Old (original cost)		xx

INTANGIBLES

General Characteristics

Lack physical substance

Uncertain benefit period

Associated with legal rights

Initial Accounting

Capitalize costs of purchasing intangibles

Expense costs of developing intangibles internally

Capitalize costs of preparing for use

    Legal fees

    Registration fees

Amortization

Straight-line amortization

Amortized over **shorter** of:

    Legal life

    Useful life

Units of sales amortization used if greater than straight-line

Tested for impairment when events suggest undiscounted future cash flow will be less than carrying value of intangible – written down to fair market value.

Intangibles with no clear legal or useful life (trademarks, perpetual franchises) must be examined annually for impairment either qualitatively or quantitatively. If impairment is likely, proceed to impairment test and write down whenever fair market value is less than carrying value.

Goodwill

Acquisition

Must be part of (an acquisition) business combination

Excess of acquisition price over fair value of underlying net assets

Internal costs

May incur development or maintenance costs

All costs are expensed

Amortization

No amortization recorded

Impairment

Annually, qualitatively (or quantitatively) assess whether it is more likely than not that the fair value of a reporting unit is less than its carrying value. If so, perform the two-step impairment test:

1. Calculate and compare the fair value of the reporting unit to its carrying value

    a. If carrying value exceeds fair value, proceed to step 2

2. Compare the implied fair value of the reporting unit goodwill to the carrying value

    a. Goodwill written down whenever implied fair value is less than carrying value

IFRS: Property, Plant, and Equipment

- Elect either Cost or Revaluation model (RM). If choose RM

    - Carrying amount = the fair value at date of revaluation less subsequent accumulated depreciation and subsequent accumulated impairment loss
    - Only for assets with value that can be reliably measured
    - Entire class of assets
    - Write asset up or down revaluation surplus account in OCI
    - Can reverse impairment loss

        - Cost method: reversal to income
        - RM: reversal to OCI

    - Requires component depreciation (e.g., parts of an airplane) and review of residual value and useful life each period

Leasehold Improvements

Amortize over shorter of:

- Useful life
- Remaining term of lease

Patents

Legal costs of defending a patent

- Successful – capitalize legal costs as addition to carrying value of patent
- Unsuccessful – recognize legal costs as expense and consider writing down patent

Research and Development (R & D)

Research – aimed at discovery of new knowledge

New product or process

Improvement to existing product or process

Development – converting new knowledge into plan or design

R & D assets:

Used for general R & D activities

Capitalize if purchased from others and alternative future uses exist

Amortized if capitalized

Charge to R & D expense

Used for specific project

Charge to R & D expense

IFRS allows capitalization of development costs if six criteria are met

Startup Costs

Costs associated with startup of organization should be immediately expensed

Franchises

Initial fee – generally capitalized and amortized

Subsequent payments – generally recognized as expense in period incurred

Software

Expense – cost up to technological feasibility

Capitalize and amortize – costs from technological feasibility to start of production

- Coding and testing
- Production of masters

Charge to inventory – costs incurred during production

Software (continued)

Time line:

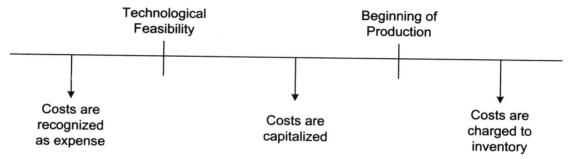

Software (continued)

Amortization of capitalized software costs – larger of:

Straight-line or **Ratio**

$$\frac{\text{Carrying value}}{\text{Remaining useful life}}$$

(Current period + future periods)

$$\frac{\text{Current revenues} \times \text{Carrying value}}{\text{Estimated remaining revenues}}$$

(Current revenues + future revenues)

Additional amortization:

Carrying value (after amortization) > Net realizable value (based on future revenues)

Excess is additional amortization

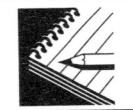

Bank Reconciliation

Bank balance
- \+ Deposits in transit
- − Outstanding checks
- ± Errors made by bank
- = Corrected balance

Book balance

Amounts collected by bank +
Unrecorded bank charges −
Errors made when recording transactions ±
Corrected balance =

| Must be equal |

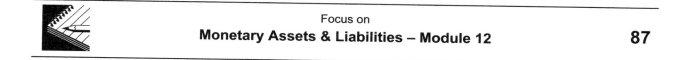

Accounts Receivable

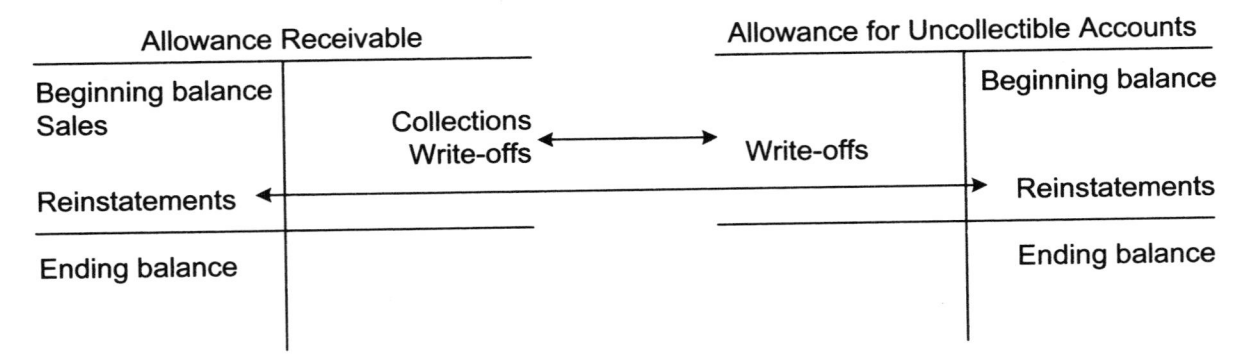

Allowance Receivable		Allowance for Uncollectible Accounts
Beginning balance		Beginning balance
Sales	Collections	
	Write-offs ⟷ Write-offs	
Reinstatements ←		→ Reinstatements
Ending balance		Ending balance

Net realizable value = Accounts receivable – Allowance for Uncollectible Accounts

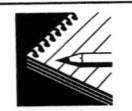

Uncollectible Accounts

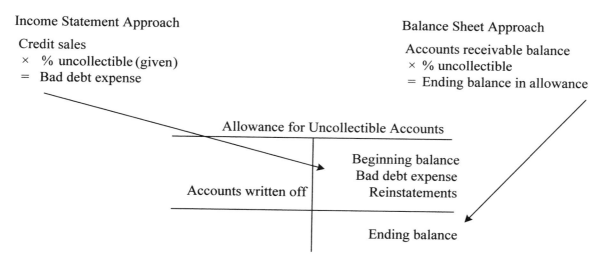

Income Statement Approach

Credit sales
× % uncollectible (given)
= Bad debt expense

Balance Sheet Approach

Accounts receivable balance
× % uncollectible
= Ending balance in allowance

Allowance for Uncollectible Accounts

Accounts written off	Beginning balance
	Bad debt expense
	Reinstatements
	Ending balance

Calculate expense and plug balance **or** calculate balance and plug expense

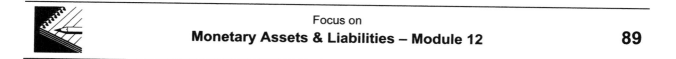

Uncollectible Accounts (continued)

Allowance Methods - GAAP

Matching concept – Bad debt expense in period of sale

Measurement concept – Accounts receivable at net realizable value

Direct Write-off Method – Non-GAAP

Violates matching concept – Bad debt expense when account written off

Violates measurement concept – Accounts receivable overstated at gross amount

Notes Received for Cash

Calculating Payment

Principal amount ÷ Present value factor = Payment amount

    Present value factor for annuity based on number of payments and interest rate

Allocating Payments

Payment amount − Interest = Principal reduction

Calculating Interest

Beginning balance
× Interest rate
× Period up to payment
= Interest up to payment

Balance after principal reduction
× Interest rate
× Period up to payment to year-end
= Interest for remainder of year

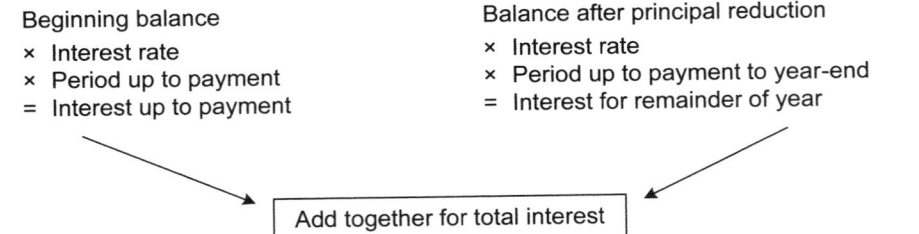

Add together for total interest

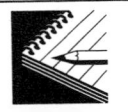

Notes Received for Goods or Services

Note Balance

Short-term: Amount = Face value

Long-term: Amount = Fair value of goods or services

Present value of payments if fair value not known

Journal entry:

Note receivable - Face amount (given)	xxx	
Revenue - Calculated amount		xxx
Discount on note receivable (plug)		xxx

Notes Received for Goods or Services

Interest Income

Face amount of note
- − Unamortized discount
- = Carrying value of note
- × Interest rate
- = Interest income

Journal entry:

Discount on note receivable	xxx	
Interest income		xxx

Financing Receivables — Discounting

Proceeds from Discounting

Face amount
+ Interest income (Face × Interest rate × Term)
= Maturity value
− Discount (Maturity value × Discount rate × Remaining term)
= Proceeds

Financing Receivables — Assignment

Treated as loan

Cash—Proceeds (given)	xxx	
Note payable secured by receivables		xxx
Accounts receivable assigned	xxx	
Accounts receivable (balance)		xxx

Financing Receivables — Factoring

Factoring without Recourse

Treated as a sale

Cash (Accounts receivable balance less fee less holdback)	xxx
Due from factor (holdback)*	xxx
Loss on sale (fee charged by the factor)	xxx
Accounts receivable (balance)	xxx

* Due from factor (receivable) is an amount the factor holds back in case customers return merchandise to the business selling the receivables. If customers return the merchandise, they will not be paying the factor.

Financing with Recourse

Treated as a sale

Cash (Accounts receivable balance less fee less holdback)	xxx	
Due from factor (holdback)	xxx	
Loss on sale (fee charged by the factor + recourse value)	xxx	
Accounts receivable (balance)		xxx
Recourse liability*		

* *The recourse liability is assigned a fair value and initially increases the loss. If receivables are 100% collected by the factor, the recourse will be reversed:*

Recourse liability	xxx	
Loss on sale		xxx

Financial Statement Analysis

Ratios Involving Current Assets & Liabilities

Working capital = current assets − current liabilities

Current ratio = current assets ÷ current liabilities

Quick ratio = quick assets ÷ current liabilities

    Quick assets − current assets readily convertible into cash

- Cash
- Accounts receivable
- Investments in trading securities

Ratios Involving Receivables

Accounts receivable turnover = Credit sales ÷ Average accounts receivable

Days to collect accounts receivable = 365 ÷ Accounts receivable turnover

or

Days to collect accounts receivable = Average accounts receivable ÷ Average sales/day

    Average sales/day = Credit sales ÷ 365

Ratios Involving Inventories

Inventory turnover = Cost of sales ÷ Average inventory

Days sales in inventory = 365 ÷ Inventory turnover

or

Days sales in inventory = Average inventory ÷ Average inventory sold/day

Average inventory sold/day = Cost of sales ÷ 365

Other Ratios

Operating cycle = Days to collect accounts receivable + Days sales in inventory

Debt to total assets = Total debt ÷ Total assets

Debt to equity = Total debt ÷ Total stockholders' equity

Return on assets = Net income ÷ Average total assets

Accounts Payable

Purchase shipment terms	Payable already recorded	Payable not already recorded
Shipping point	No adjustment	Adjust – add
Destination	Adjust – deduct	No adjustment

Contingencies

Loss Contingencies

Probable – Accrue & disclose

- Not estimable – Disclose only
- Estimable within range – Accrue minimum of range

Reasonably possible – Disclose only

Remote – Neither accrued nor disclosed

Contingencies and Provisions

IFRS

Distinguishes between contingencies and provisions

- Contingencies depend upon some future event and are disclosed only

Provisions are liabilities that are uncertain in timing or amount

- Probability threshold is 50%—accrue and disclose
- Estimable within a range—accrue the midpoint of the range

Gain Contingencies

Never accrue (until realization occurs or is assured beyond reasonable doubt)

May disclose

Estimated & Accrued Amounts

Money 1st – Goods or services 2nd

- Expenses – prepaid
- Revenues – unearned

Goods or services 1st – Money 2nd

- Expenses – accrued
- Revenues – receivable

Revenue Items

Calculate amount earned or amount collected

1) Determine changes in accrual items:

	Debit	Credit
Revenue receivable	Increase	Decrease
Unearned revenue	Decrease	Increase

2) Prepare journal entry

Cash	xxx		
Revenue receivable	xxx	or	xxx
Unearned revenue	xxx	or	xxx
Revenues			xxx

3) If amount collected is given, that is the debit to cash and the amount required to balance the entry is the amount earned. If the amount earned is given, that is the credit to revenues and the amount required to balance the entry is the amount collected.

Expense Items

Calculate amount incurred or amount paid

1) Determine changes in accrual items:

	Debit	Credit
Prepaid expense	Increase	Decrease
Accrued expense	Decrease	Increase

2) Prepare journal entry

Expense	xxx		
Prepaid expense	xxx	or	xxx
Accrued expense	xxx	or	xxx
Cash			xxx

3) If amount paid is given, that is the credit to cash and the amount required to balance the entry is the amount incurred. If the amount incurred is given, that is the debit to expense and the amount required to balance the entry is the amount paid.

Insurance

Prepaid insurance (end of year)

  Total premiums paid × Months remaining / Total # of months

Insurance expense

  Prepaid insurance (beginning) + Premiums paid − Prepaid insurance (ending)

Royalties

Royalty income for current year

1st payment – includes royalties earned in latter part of previous period early in current period

- Include payment
- Deduct royalties from previous period

2nd payment – received for royalties earned during current period

- Include entire payment

Additional royalties

- Add royalties earned for latter part of current period

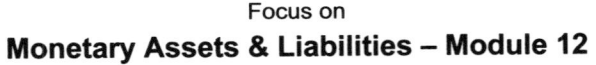

Service Contract

Service contract revenues – fees received uniformly during period

Fees received
× % earned in 1st period
× 50%

Deferred service contract revenues

Fees received
− Service contract revenues

Coupons

Discounts on merchandise

Number of coupons not expired

× % expected to be redeemed

× Cost per coupon (face + service fee)
− Amount already paid
= Liability

Premiums (Prizes)

Number of units sold

× % expected to be redeemed
÷ number required per prize
− Prizes already sent
× Cost per prize

= Liability

Warranties*

Warranty expense

Sales
× % of warranty costs
= Expense for period ─────────────────────┐

Warranty liability

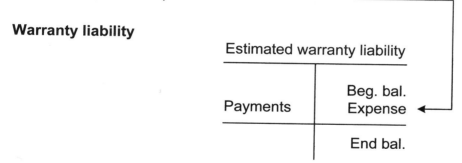

Estimated warranty liability

Payments | Beg. bal.
Expense ◄───┘

End bal.

* *When calculating warranty expense, be sure to apply the matching principle (e.g., Expected returns on year 1 sales = 2% in year of sale and 3% the year following the sale. Warranty expense would be calculated using 5%, matching all expenses to the period of the sale).*

Compensated Absences

Four conditions:

- Past services of employees
- Amounts vest or accumulate
- Probable
- Estimable

When all conditions met:

	Vest	**Accumulate**
Vacation pay	Must accrue	Must accrue
Sick pay	Must accrue	May accrue

Miscellaneous Liabilities

Refinancing Liabilities

To exclude from current liabilities – 2 requirements:

- Company intends to refinance on a long-term basis
- Company can demonstrate ability to refinance

The ability to refinance can be demonstrated in either of 2 ways:

- Refinance on long-term basis after balance sheet date but before issuance
- Enter into firm agreement with lender having ability to provide long-term financing

IFRS:

- Must have an agreement in place by the balance sheet date to exclude from current liabilities

ACCOUNTING FOR LEASES

Lessee Reporting

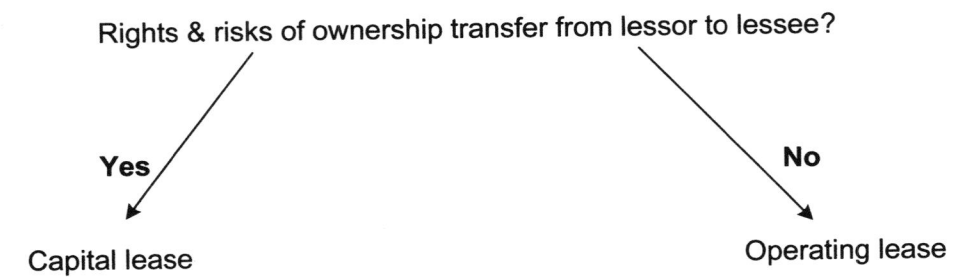

Rights & risks of ownership transfer from lessor to lessee?

Yes

Capital lease

No

Operating lease

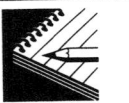

Transfer of rights & risks of ownership – At least 1 of 4 criteria

Actual transfer

- Title transfers to lessee by end of term
- Lease contains bargain purchase option

Transfer in substance

- Lease term ≥ 75% of useful life
- Present value of min lease payments ≥ 90% of fair market value

To calculate present value – lessee uses lower of:

- Incremental borrowing rate
- Rate implicit in lease (if known)

Capital Leases

Inception of lease

Journal entry to record lease:

Leased asset	xxx	
Lease obligation		xxx

Amount of asset & liability = PV of minimum lease payments:

- Payments beginning at inception result in annuity due
- Payments beginning at end of first year result in ordinary annuity
- Payments include bargain purchase option or guaranteed residual value (lump sum at end of lease)

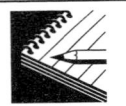

Lease payments

Payment at inception:

Lease obligation	xxx	
Cash		xxx

Subsequent payments:

Interest expense	xxx	
Lease obligation	xxx	
Cash		xxx

Interest amount:

Balance in lease obligation
- ×   Interest rate (used to calculate PV)
- ×   Time since last payment (usually 1 year)
- =   Interest amount

Periodic Expenses - Depreciation

Actual transfer (1 of first 2 criteria)

- Life = useful life of property
- Salvage value taken into consideration

Transfer in substance (1 of latter 2 criteria)

- Life = shorter of useful life or lease term
- No salvage value

Periodic Expenses – Executory costs

Consist of insurance, maintenance, & taxes

Recognized as expense when incurred

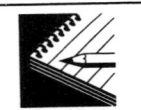

Balance Sheet Presentation

Leased asset

- Reported as P, P, & E
- Reported net of accumulated depreciation

Lease obligation

- Current liability = Principal payments due in subsequent period
- Noncurrent liability = Remainder

Disclosures

- Amount of assets recorded under capital leases
- Minimum lease payments for each of next 5 years and in aggregate
- Description of leasing activities

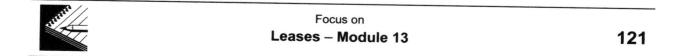

Lessor Reporting

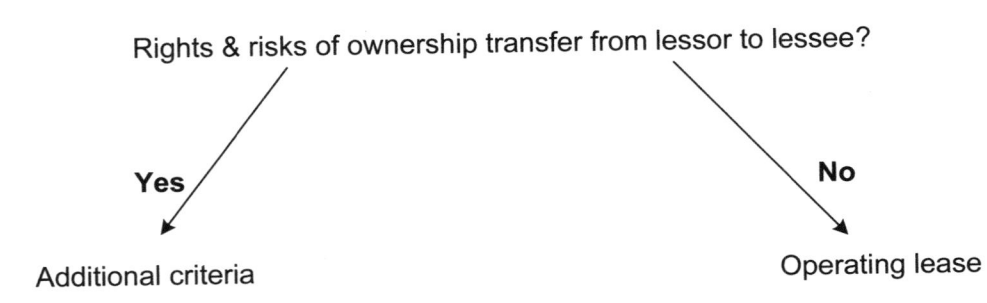

Rights & risks of ownership transfer from lessor to lessee?

Yes → Additional criteria

No → Operating lease

Transfer of rights & risks of ownership – At least 1 of 4 criteria

- Same criteria as lessee
- To calculate present value – lessor uses rate implicit in lease

---

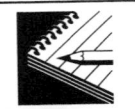

Additional Criteria

- Collectibility of lease payments reasonably predictable
- No significant uncertainties as to costs to be incurred in connection with lease

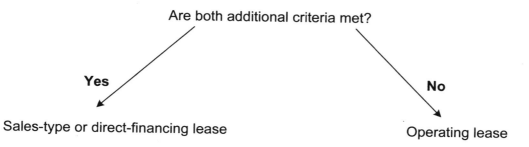

Are both additional criteria met?

Yes

Sales-type or direct-financing lease

No

Operating lease

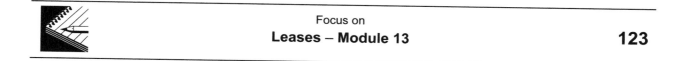

Sales-Type & Direct-Financing Leases

Inception of lease

Journal entry to record lease:

Receivable	xxx	
Accumulated depreciation (if any)	xxx	
Asset		xxx
Gain (if any)		xxx

Receivable = fair value of property & present value of lease payments (rate implicit in lease)

Asset & accum dep – To remove carrying value of asset from lessor's books

Gain

- If amount needed to balance the entry, it is a gain or loss and this is a sales-type lease
- If the entry balances without a gain or loss, this is a direct financing lease

Collections

At inception of lease:

Cash	xxx	
Receivable		xxx

Subsequent collections:

Cash	xxx	
Interest income (formula)		xxx
Receivable		xxx

Interest amount:

Balance of receivable
× Interest rate (implicit in lease)
× Time since last payment (usually 1 year)
= Interest amount

Balance Sheet Presentation

Receivable

- Current asset – Principal collections due within one year
- Noncurrent asset – Remainder

Operating Leases

Lessor Accounting

Rent revenue

Various expenses (depreciation on asset, taxes, insurance, & maintenance)

Lessee Accounting

Rent expense

Miscellaneous expenses (taxes, insurance, & maintenance)

Rent revenue or expense

- Recognized uniformly over lease
- Total of rents over term of lease ÷ Number of periods = Rent per period

Sale-Leaseback Transactions

Minor Leaseback

Leaseback ≤ 10% of fair value of property sold

- Sale and leaseback recognized as separate transactions
- Gain or loss on sale

Other Leasebacks

Seller-lessee retains significant portion of property

- Some or all of gain deferred
- Deferred amount limited to present value of leaseback payments
- Deferred amount spread over lease
- Remainder recognized in period of sale

IFRS Lease Rules

- IFRS: Lease classification by lessee/lessor the same. Key issue: Look at economic substance to determine if substantially all benefits/risks of ownership transferred
- Two types of leases: Finance or operating
- IFRS: If sale followed by operating lease, recognize all gain. If sale followed by financial lease, defer and amortize gain
- IFRS: Must bifurcate land and building

  - Four tests any one of which means it is a finance lease. Note: No 75% or 90% test
  - The lease transfers ownership to the lessee by the end of the lease term or the lease contains a bargain purchase option, and it is reasonably certain that the option will be exercised.
  - The lease term is for the major part of the economic life of the asset
  - The present value of the minimum lease payments at the inception of the lease is at least equal to substantially all of the fair value of the leased asset.
  - The leased assets are of a specialized nature such that only the lessee can use them without modifications.

BONDS

Issuance – Interest date

Cash (present value approach)	xxx		
Discount or premium (plug)	xxx	or	xxx
Bonds payable (face amount)			xxx

Issuance – Between interest dates

Cash (sales price approach + interest amount)	xxx		
Discount or premium (plug)	xxx	or	xxx
Interest payable (interest amount)			xxx
Bonds payable (face)			xxx

Proceeds

Present value approach

      Present value of principal (lump sum) at yield rate

  +   Present value of interest (ordinary annuity) at yield rate

Sales price approach

- Sales price given as percentage of face amount
- Multiplied by face to give proceeds amount

Interest

Bond issued between interest dates

Calculated amount

    Face amount of bonds

    ×   Stated rate

    ×   Portion of year since previous interest date

    =   Interest amount

Effective interest method - GAAP

Interest payable
   Face amount
× Stated rate
× Portion of year since
   previous interest date
= Interest payable

Interest expense
   Carrying value
× Yield rate
× Portion of year since
   previous interest date
= Interest expense

Difference
Amortization of discount or premium

Straight-line method – Not GAAP

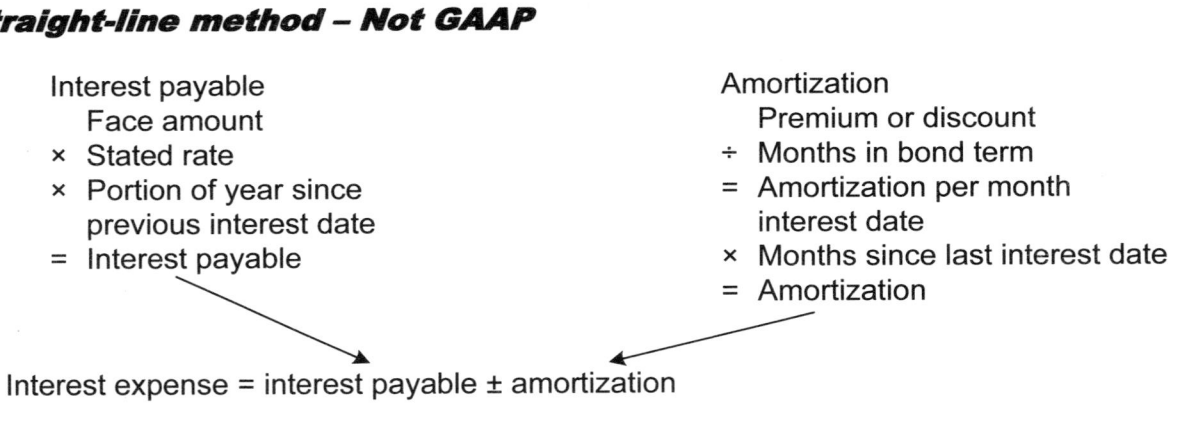

Interest payable
   Face amount
- × Stated rate
- × Portion of year since previous interest date
- = Interest payable

Amortization
   Premium or discount
- ÷ Months in bond term
- = Amortization per month interest date
- × Months since last interest date
- = Amortization

Interest expense = interest payable ± amortization

- • + Amortization of discount
- • – Amortization of premium

Recording Interest Expense

Interest expense	xxx		
Bond premium or discount (amortization)	xxx	or	xxx
Cash or interest payable			xxx

Bond Issue Costs

Recorded as asset

- Deferred charge
- Amortized (straight-line) over term of bond
- Not considered part of carrying value

Bond Retirement

Bond payable (face amount)	xxx	
Bond premium or discount (balance)	xxx or	xxx
Gain or loss (plug)	xxx or	xxx
Bond issue costs (balance)		xxx
Cash (amount paid)		xxx

Gain or loss is extraordinary if retirement is determined to be both unusual and infrequent

---

Convertible Bonds

Recorded as bonds that are not convertible

Upon conversion:

Book Value Method			
Bonds payable (face)	xx		
Prem or disc (bal)	xx	or	xx
Com stk (par)			xx
APIC (diff)			xx

Market Value Method			
Bonds payable (face)	xx		
Prem or disc (bal)	xx	or	xx
Com stk (par)			xx
APIC (computed)			xx
Gain or loss (diff)		xx	or	xx

Book value method

- Issuance price of stock = Carrying value of bonds
- No gain or loss

Market value method

- Issue price of stock = Fair market value
- Gain or loss recognized

Detachable Warrants

Allocate proceeds using relative fair value method

    Fair value of bonds (without warrants)
+   Fair value of warrants (without bonds)
=   Total fair value

Bonds = Proceeds × Value of bonds/total value

Warrants = Proceeds × Value of warrants/total value

Record issuance:

Cash (total proceeds)	xx	
Discount or premium (plug*)	xx or xx	
APIC (amount allocated to warrants)		xx
Bonds payable (face amount)		xx

* Bonds payable − Discount or plus premium = Amount allocated to bonds

Disclosures

A bond issuer should disclose:

- The face amount of bonds
- The nature and terms of the bonds including a discussion of credit and market risk, cash requirements, and related accounting policies
- The fair value of the bonds at the balance sheet date, indicated as a reasonable estimate of fair value

IFRS

- Option to value financial liabilities at fair value
- Financial instruments with characteristics of both debt and equity: "Compound instruments."

  - Convertible bonds and bonds with detachable warrants separated into components of debt and equity
  - Record liability component at fair value
  - Plug remaining value assigned to equity component

TROUBLED DEBT RESTRUCTURING

Transfer property to creditor

Liability (amount forgiven)	xxx	
Gain or loss on disposal	xxx or	xxx
Asset (carrying value)		xxx
Gain on restructure		xxx

Gain (or loss) on disposal = Fair value of asset – Carrying value of asset

Gain on restructure = Carrying value of debt – Fair value of asset

Issuance of equity

Liability (amount forgiven)	xxx	
Common stock (par value)		xxx
APIC (based on fair value)		xxx
Gain on restructure		xxx

APIC = Fair value of stock issued – Par value of stock issued

Gain on restructure = Fair value of stock – Carrying value of debt

Modification of Terms

Total payments under new terms:

- If ≥ carrying value of debt – no adjustment made
- If < carrying value of debt – difference is gain

Treatment of restructuring gain

Reported in ordinary income unless it is determined that the restructuring is both unusual and infrequent.

Bankruptcy

Order of distribution:

1) Fully secured creditors

    - Receive payment in full
    - Excess of fair value of asset over debt added to remaining available money

2) Partially secured creditors

    - Receive payment equal to fair value of collateral
    - Difference considered unsecured debt

3) Unsecured creditors

    - All receive partial payment
    - Remaining available money ÷ Total of unsecured claims = Ratio
    - Ratio multiplied by each claim to determine payment

PENSION PLANS

Pension Expense

Service cost (debit)

+ Interest (debit

– Actual return on plan assets (CPA exam assumes positive returns, so credit)

+ Unexpected losses (credit) /unexpected gains (debit)

± Amortization of prior service cost (debit)

± Corridor amortization of gains (credit) or losses (debit) in Accumulated Other Comprehensive Income (AOCI)

= Pension expense reported in operating income

Pension Expense (continued)

Service cost – Increase in plan's projected benefit obligation (PBO) resulting from services performed by employees

Interest – Beginning PBO × discount (interest) rate

Actual return on plan assets – Increase in plan assets after eliminating contributions and adding back distributions

Gains or losses – 2 components

- Difference between actual return and expected return
- Amortization of AOCI for Gains/Losses in amount when beginning balance > greater of 10% of beginning PBO or 10% of market related value of beginning plan assets

Report on Balance Sheet difference between fair value of plan assets and the PBO as a noncurrent asset if overfunded and a noncurrent liability if underfunded in a pension asset/liability account.

Disclosures

- Description of funding policies and types of assets held: equity, debt, real estate and other
- Six components of Pension expense for the period
- Expected benefits to be paid each of the next five years and in aggregate for the following five years
- Expected cash contribution for the following year

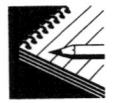

IFRS Pension Accounting

- IFRS: Can choose to recognize all gains or losses in other comprehensive income (i.e., avoid the corridor approach; corridor approach eliminated for firms with fiscal year ends after January 1, 2013)
- IFRS: Do not have to report (un)funded status of postemployment plans on face of balance sheet
- IFRS: Requires actual fair value of assets (i.e., no weighted-average)
- IFRS: May present different elements of pension expense in different parts of income statement (e.g., interest expense in financing section of income statement and service cost in operating income).

POSTRETIREMENT BENEFITS

Types of Benefits

Company pays for:

- Health care
- Tuition assistance
- Legal services
- Life insurance
- Day care
- Housing subsidies

Individuals covered:

- Retired employees
- Beneficiaries
- Covered dependents

Postretirement Benefit Expense

Service cost (debit)

+   Interest (debit)

−   Actual return on plan assets (CPA exam assumes positive returns, so credit)

+   Unexpected losses (credit) /unexpected gains (debit)

±   Amortization of prior service cost (debit)

±   Corridor amortization of gains (credit) or losses (debit) in Accumulated Other Comprehensive Income (AOCI)

=   Postretirement benefit expense

ACCOUNTING FOR INCOME TAXES
(ASC 740/FAS 109)

Income Tax Expense

Taxable income = Pretax accounting income

- No temporary differences
- Income tax expense = Current income tax expense
- No deferred tax effect

Taxable income ≠ Pretax accounting income

- Temporary differences
- Income tax expense = Current income tax expense ± Deferred income taxes

Current Income Tax

Current income tax expense = Taxable income × Current tax rate

Current tax liability = Current income tax expense − Estimated payments

Taxable income:

> Pretax accounting income (financial statement income)
± Permanent differences
± Changes in cumulative amounts of temporary differences .
= Taxable income

Permanent & Temporary Differences

Permanent differences

- Nontaxable income (interest income on municipal bonds) & nondeductible expenses (premiums on officers' life insurance)
- No income tax effect

Temporary differences

- Carrying values of assets or liabilities $\neq$ tax bases
- May be taxable temporary differences (TTD) or deductible temporary differences (DTD)
- Temporary taxable differences result in deferred tax liabilities and temporary deductible differences result in deferred tax assets

Assets

Financial statement basis $>$ tax basis $=$ TTD
Financial statement basis $<$ tax basis $=$ DTD

Permanent & Temporary Differences (continued)

Liabilities

    Financial statement basis > tax basis = DTD

    Financial statement basis < tax basis = TTD

- Often, it is easier to examine the net effect on income. For example, if straight-line depreciation is used for financial statement purposes and MACRS for tax purposes, depreciation expense for book purposes < that for tax purposes leading to net financial income > net taxable income resulting in a deferred tax liability.

    - Net financial income > net taxable income = deferred tax liability
    - Net financial income < net taxable income = deferred tax asset

Deferred Tax Assets & Liabilities

TTD × Enacted future tax rate = Deferred tax liability

DTD × Enacted future tax rate = Deferred tax asset

Selecting appropriate rate:

1) Determine future period when temporary difference will have tax effect (period of reversal)
2) Determine enacted tax rate for that period

Deferred Tax Asset Valuation Allowance

May apply to any deferred tax asset

- Is it more likely than not that some or all of deferred tax asset will not be realized
- Consider tax planning strategies

Valuation allowance = portion of deferred tax asset that will not be realized

Deferred Income Tax Expense or Benefit

1) Calculate balances of deferred tax liabilities and assets and valuation allowances
2) Combine into single net amount
3) Compare to combined amount at beginning of period

- Increase in net liability amount = deferred income tax expense
- Decrease in net asset amount = deferred income tax expense
- Increase in net asset amount = deferred income tax benefit
- Decrease in net liability amount = deferred income tax benefit

Balance Sheet Presentation

Identify current and noncurrent deferred tax assets, liabilities, and valuation allowances

Current – TTD or DTD relates to asset or liability classified as current

Noncurrent – TTD or DTD relates to asset or liability classified as noncurrent

TTD or DTD does not relate to specific asset or liability (such as result of net operating loss carryforward) – classify as current or noncurrent depending on period of tax effect

1) Combine current deferred tax assets, liabilities, and valuation allowances into single amount
2) Report as current deferred tax asset or liability
3) Combine noncurrent deferred tax assets, liabilities, and valuation allowances into single amount
4) Report as noncurrent deferred tax asset or liability

IFRS for Deferred Income Taxes

- Deferred tax assets/liabilities always noncurrent
- Use enacted rate or substantially enacted rate
- No valuation allowance (reported net)

Accounting for Uncertainty in Income Taxes

- Applies to all tax positions related to income taxes subject to ASC 740/FAS 109
- Utilizes a two-step approach for evaluating tax positions.

  - Recognition (Step 1) occurs when an enterprise concludes that a tax position, based solely on its technical merits, is more likely than not to be sustained upon examination.

  - Measurement (Step 2) is only addressed if Step 1 has been maintained. Under Step 2, the tax benefit is measured as the largest amount of benefit, determined on a cumulative probability basis, that is more likely than not to be realized (i.e., a likelihood of occurrence greater than 50%).

Accounting for Uncertainty in Income Taxes (continued)

- Those tax positions failing to qualify for initial recognition under Step 1 are recognized in the first subsequent interim period that they meet the more-likely-than-not standard, and are resolved through negotiation or litigation or on expiration of the statute of limitations.
- Derecognition of a tax position that was previously recognized occurs when the item fails to meet more-likely-than-not threshold.
- ASC 740/FIN 48 specifically prohibits the use of a deferred tax valuation allowance as a substitute for derecognition of tax positions.

STOCKHOLDERS' EQUITY

Issuance of Common Stock

Stock issued for cash, property, or services:

Journal entry:

Cash, property, or expense (fair value)	xxx	
Common stock (par or stated value)		xxx
APIC (difference)		xxx

Common Stock Subscribed

Subscription – Journal entry:

Cash (down payment)	xxx	
Subscriptions receivable (balance)	xxx	
Common stock subscribed (par or stated value)		xxx
APIC (difference)		xxx

Collection and issuance of shares – Journal entries:

Cash (balance)	xxx	
Subscriptions receivable		xxx
Common stock subscribed (par or stated value)	xxx	
Common stock (par or stated value)		xxx

Treasury Stock

Acquisition of shares:

Cost Method

TS (cost)	xx	
Cash		xx

Par Value Method

TS (par value)	xx
APIC (original amount)	xx
RE (difference)	xx

or

APIC from TS (difference)	xx
Cash (cost)	xx

Acquisition of shares (continued)

Sale – more than cost:

Cost Method		
Cash (proceeds)	xx	
TS (cost)		xx
APIC from TS		xx

Par Value Method		
Cash (proceeds)	xx	
TS (par)		xx
APIC (difference)		xx

Sale – less than cost:

Cost Method		
Cash (proceeds)	xx	
APIC from TS (difference up to balance)	xx	
RE (remainder of difference)	xx	
TS (cost)		xx

Par Value Method

Same entry as above

Characteristics of Preferred Stock

Preference over common stock

- Receive dividends prior to common stockholders
- **Paid before common on liquidation**

Cumulative preferred stock

- Unpaid dividends accumulated as dividends in arrears
- Paid in subsequent periods prior to payment of current dividends to common or preferred
- Not considered liability until declared

Participating preferred stock

- Receive current dividends prior to common stockholders
- Receive additional dividends, in proportion to common stockholders, in periods of high dividends

Equity Instruments with Characteristics of Liabilities

Financial instruments shares should be classified as liabilities on the balance sheet, even when they appear to be in the form of equity, when any of these characteristics apply:

- Preferred shares have a mandatory redemption date payable in cash
- An obligation exists to repurchase shares through the transfer of assets to the shareholder.
- Shares are convertible to other shares when the exchange rate is based on a fixed monetary value of issuer shares or is tied to variations in the fixed value of something other than the issuer's shares.

Note that convertible shares whose conversion rate is not adjusted for changes in values do not fall into this category (e.g. preferred stock convertible at a fixed 10 for 1 ratio to the common stock would not be a liability)

Dividends

Cash Dividends

Recorded when declared

1) Dividends in arrears to preferred stockholders if cumulative
2) Normal current dividend to preferred stockholders
3) Comparable current dividend to common stockholders
4) Remainder

   - Allocated between common and preferred shares if preferred stock is participating
   - Paid to common stockholders if preferred stock is nonparticipating

Property Dividends

Journal entry

Retained earnings (fmv of property)	xxx	
Gain (or loss)	xxx or	xxx
Asset (carrying value of property)		xxx

Liquidating Dividends

Journal entry

Retained earnings (balance)	xxx	
APIC (plug)	xxx	
Cash or Dividends payable		xxx

Stock Dividends

Journal entry – Normal stock dividend – usually 20% or less

Retained earnings (fmv of stock issued)	xxx	
Common stock (par or stated value)		xxx
APIC (difference)		xxx

Journal entry – Large stock dividend – usually more than 25% – referred to as stock split affected in the form of a stock dividend

Retained earnings (par or stated value)	xxx	
Common stock (par or stated value)		xxx

Preferred Stock – Special Issuances

Preferred with Detachable Warrants

Cash (proceeds)	xxx	
APIC from warrants (amount allocated)		xxx
Preferred stock (par)		xxx
APIC from preferred stock (difference)		xxx

Amount allocated to warrants using relative fair value method:

    Fair value of warrants

+   Fair value of stock

=   Total fair value

Allocation:

- Fair value of warrants ÷ Total fair value × Proceeds = Amount allocated to warrants
- Fair value of stock ÷ Total fair value × Proceeds = Amount allocated to stock

Convertible Preferred Stock

Journal entry – Issuance

Cash (proceeds)	xxx	
Preferred stock (par)		xxx
APIC from preferred stock (difference)		xxx

Journal entry – Conversion

Preferred stock (par)	xxx	
APIC from preferred stock (original amount)	xxx	
Common stock (par or stated value)		xxx
APIC (difference)		xxx

Retained Earnings

Appropriations

Set up to disclose to financial statement users future commitments that are not subject to accrual.

Journal entry:

Retained earnings	xxx	
Retained earnings appropriated for…		xxx

When the commitment is met, accrued, or avoided, the appropriation is reversed.

Journal entry:

Retained earnings appropriated for…	xxx	
Retained earnings		xxx

Prior Period Adjustments

Made to correct errors in financial statements of prior periods

Adjustment to beginning retained earnings

- Equal to net amount of errors from periods prior to earliest period presented
- Reduced by tax effect

Presented on statement of retained earnings

- Unadjusted beginning balance reported
- Increased or decreased for prior period adjustment
- Result is adjusted beginning balance

Statement of Retained Earnings

	Beginning retained earnings, as previously reported	xxx
±	Prior period adjustments	<u>xxx</u>
=	Beginning retained earnings, as adjusted	xxx
+	Net income for period	xxx
−	Dividends	xxx
−	Appropriations	xxx
+	Appropriations eliminated	<u>xxx</u>
=	Ending retained earnings	<u>xxx</u>

IFRS and Owner's Equity

- Unlike US GAAP, statement of changes in owners' equity required

Stock Options Plans

Noncompensatory Plans

Noncompensatory when:

- All employees participate
- Participation uniform among employees
- Option period limited to reasonable time
- Discount below market price limited to reasonable amount

Compensatory Plans

Journal entry

Deferred compensation	xxx
APIC – Options	xxx

Options must be accounted for using FMV at date of grant based on:

- Market price of options with similar characteristics
- Option pricing model

  - Binomial distribution model
  - Black-Scholes model

- Intrinsic value (stock price – exercise price) only used when FMV cannot be determined at grant date and must be replaced by FMV as soon as estimate is available

Compensation recognized over service period

IFRS and Stock Options

- Applies to all share-based payments
- Requires fair-value method in all cases
- Measurement of deferred tax asset is based on estimate of future tax deduction at end of each period.

  - Changes in stock prices change to deferred tax asset
  - Excess tax benefits (windfalls) are recorded first in equity (up to amount of cumulative book compensation expense) and then in equity
  - Shortfalls become income tax expense
  - Excess tax benefits are reported as cash inflows from operations all ESOPs are compensatory

Stock Appreciation Rights

Calculating liability

> Stock price
> - Amount specified in stock appreciation rights
> = Amount per share
> × # of stock appreciation rights
> = Total liability
> × Portion of service period elapsed
> = Liability on balance sheet date

Amount needed to increase or decrease liability is recognized as compensation expense

Quasi Reorganizations

Journal entry:

Common stock (reduction in par value)	xxx		
APIC (plug)	xxx or	xxx	
Retained earnings (eliminate deficit)		xxx	
Assets (eliminate overstatements)		xxx	

Book Value Per Share

Calculation:

Total stockholders' equity
- − Preferred stock (par value or liquidation preference)
- − Dividends in arrears on cumulative preferred stock
- = Stockholders' equity attributable to common stockholders
- ÷ Common shares outstanding at balance sheet date
- = Book value per common share

Disclosure of Information about Capital Structure

Rights & privileges of various debt & equity securities outstanding

- Number of shares of common and preferred stock authorized, issued, & outstanding
- Dividend & liquidation preferences
- Participation rights
- Call prices & dates
- Conversion or exercise prices or rates & pertinent dates
- Sinking fund requirements
- Unusual voting rights
- Significant terms of contracts to issue additional shares

Reporting Stockholders' Equity

6% cumulative preferred stock, $100 par value, 200,000 shares authorized, 120,000 shares issued and outstanding		$ 12,000,000
Common stock, $10 par value, 1,500,000 shares authorized, 1,150,000 shares issued and 1,090,000 shares outstanding		11,500,000
Additional paid-in capital		3,650,000
		27,150,000
Retained Earnings:		
Unappropriated	$ 6,925,000	
Retained earnings appropriated for plant expansion	1,400,000	8,325,000
Accumulated other comprehensive income:		
Accumulated unrealized gain due to increase		
In value of marketable securities available for sale	750,000	
Accumulated translation adjustment	(515,000)	235,000
	35,710,000	
Less: Treasury stock, 60,000 shares at cost		780,000
Total Stockholders' Equity		$ 34,930,000

Earnings Per Share

Reporting Earnings Per Share

Simple capital structure

- No potentially dilutive securities outstanding
- Present basic EPS only

Complex capital structure

- Potentially dilutive securities outstanding
- Dual presentation of EPS – basic EPS & diluted EPS

Potentially dilutive securities – Securities that can be converted into common shares

- Convertible bonds and convertible preferred stock
- Options, rights, and warrants

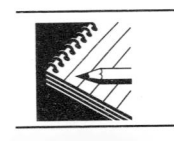

Basic EPS

Numerator

Income Available to Common Stockholders

Income from continuing operations
- − Dividends declared on noncumulative preferred stock
- − Current dividends on cumulative preferred stock (whether or not declared)
- = Income from continuing operations available to common stockholders
- ± Discontinued operations
- ± Extraordinary items
- = Net income available to common stockholders

Denominator

Weighted-average common shares outstanding on the balance sheet date

Diluted EPS

Adjust numerator & denominator for dilutive securities

- Assume conversion into common shares
- Dilutive if EPS decreases

Convertible Preferred Stock

Dilutive if basic EPS is greater than preferred dividend per share of common stock obtainable:

- Add preferred dividends back to numerator
- Add common shares that preferred would be converted into to denominator

Convertible Bonds

Dilutive if basic EPS is greater than interest, net of tax, per share of common stock obtainable:

- Add interest, net of tax, to numerator
- Add common shares that bonds would be converted into to denominator

Options, Rights, & Warrants

Dilutive when market price exceeds exercise price (proceeds from exercise)

The **treasury stock method** is applied

Number of options ⟶ Number of options
  × Exercise price
  = Proceeds from exercise
  ÷ Average market price of stock during period
  = Shares reacquired with proceeds ⟶ − Shares reacquired
                                  = Increase in denominator

Calculation done on quarter-by-quarter basis

Presentation of EPS Information

Income Statement

Simple capital structure – Basic EPS only

- Income from continuing operations
- Net income

Complex capital structure – Basic & Diluted EPS

- Income from continuing operations
- Net income

Additional Disclosures (income statement or notes)

- Discontinued operations
- Extraordinary items

METHODS OF REPORTING INVESTMENTS

Method	Conditions
Consolidation	Majority owned (> 50%)
Equity	Less than majority owned
	Ability to exercise significant influence
	Ownership generally ≥ 20%
Cost	Less than majority owned
	Unable to exercise significant influence
	Ownership generally < 20%
	Not an investment in marketable securities
Special Rules (ASC 320/FASB #115)	Less than majority owned
	Unable to exercise significant influence
	Ownership generally < 20%
	Investment in marketable securities

Equity Method

Carrying Value of Investment

Cost
+ Earnings
− Dividends
= Carrying value of investment

Earnings

Income reported by investee
× % of ownership
= Unadjusted amount
− Adjustments
= Investor's share of investee's earnings

Adjustments to Earnings

1) Compare initial investment to FMV of underlying net assets
2) Portion of excess may be due to inventory

   Deduct from income in the first year (unless inventory not sold during year)

3) Portion of excess may be due to depreciable asset

   Divide by useful life and deduct from income each year

4) Portion of excess may be due to land

   No adjustment (unless land sold during year)

5) Remainder of excess attributed to goodwill

   Test each year for impairment and deduct from income if it has occurred

Application of Equity Method

Information given:

Investment	25%
Cost	$400,000
Book value of investee's underlying net assets	$900,000
Undervalued assets:	
Inventory	100,000
Building (20 yrs)	400,000
Land	200,000
Investee's unadjusted income	$225,000
Dividends	$40,000

Application of Equity Method (continued)

Information Applied

Value of investment − $400,000 ÷ 25%		$1,6000,000
Book value of underlying net assets		900,000
Difference		$ 700,000

Reconciliation of difference			*Earnings adjustment*
Inventory	$100,000		$100,000
Building	400,000	÷20	20,000
Land	200,000		
Total	$700,000		$120,000

Earnings			*Carrying value*	
Income reported by investee	$225,000		Cost	$400,000
• Adjustments	(120,000)		+ Earnings	26,250
= Adjusted amount	105,000		− Dividends	
× % of ownership	25%		($40,000 × 25%)	10,000
= Investor's share	$ 26,250		= Carrying value	$416,250

Changes to and from the Equity Method

Equity Method to Cost Method

- No longer able to exercise significant influence
- Usually associated with sale of portion of investment
- Apply equity method to date of change
- Apply cost method from date of change

Cost Method to Equity Method

- Now able to exercise significant influence
- Usually associated with additional purchase
- Apply equity method retroactively
- Affects retained earnings and investment for prior periods

Fair Value Option

- An entity may elect to value its securities at fair value.
- If elected, available-for-sale, held-to-maturity, or equity method investments securities MTM and gain/loss goes to income

Marketable Securities (MES)

	Trading Securities	Available for Sale(AFS)	Held to Maturity (HTM)
Types of securities in classification	Debt or equity	Debt or equity	Debt only
Balance sheet classification	Current	Current or noncurrent	Noncurrent until maturity
Carrying amount on balance sheet	Fair market value	Fair market value	Cost, net of amortization
Unrealized gains and losses	Income statement	Equity section of balance sheet*	Not applicable
Realized gains and losses	Income statement	Income statement	In accordance w/amortized cost

* *Excluded from net income – included in comprehensive income*

Transferring MES between Categories

When transferring between categories (e.g., Trading to AFS), the transfer is

1. Accounted for at fair value
2. Unrealized holding gains/losses are adjusted so as not to be double counted

IFRS Investments

Similar to US GAAP, IFRS classifies securities in categories but the account titles differ

Held for Trading (HFT) — further classified as a fair value through profit or loss (FVTPL) security.

- FVTPL securities are remeasured each accounting period.
- Available for Sale (AFS)
- Held to Maturity (HTM)
- Equity method investments (can use the equity method or FVTPL)
- Can elect to use the FVTPL method for AFS or HTM securities providing the security has an active market.
- Once the election is made, it may not be changed.

Instruments **without** quoted market prices should be accounted for using the cost method.

Life Insurance

Payment of premium:

Cash surrender value of life insurance (increase in value)	xxx	
Insurance expense (plug)	xxx	
Cash (premium amount)		xxx

Death of insured:

Cash (face of policy)	xxx	
Cash surrender value of life insurance (balance)		xxx
Gain (difference)		xxx

STATEMENT OF CASH FLOWS

Purpose of Statement

Summarizes sources and uses of cash and **cash equivalents**

Classifies cash flows into operating, investing, and financing activities

Cash Equivalents

Easily converted into cash (liquid)

Original maturity ≤ 3 months

Format of Statement

Cash provided or (used) by **operating** activities
±   Cash provided or (used) by **investing** activities
±   Cash provided or (used) by **financing** activities
=   Net increase or (decrease) in cash & cash equivalents
+   Beginning balance
=   Ending balance

Inputs to the Cash Flow Statement

Each item on the balance sheet (change from prior year) and income statement must be accounted for. In general:

Operating activities:

- Income statement items/adjustments (e.g., sales)
- Current assets and current liabilities (e.g., accounts receivable)

Investing activities:

- Noncurrent assets (e.g., building)

Financial activities:

- Noncurrent liabilities and equity (e.g., bank loan, stock)

Some changes do not involve cash (equipment purchased with stock) and some do not follow the general rule (e.g., dividends payable is a current liability, but since it is the result of stock ownership, its adjustment will appear in financing activities instead of operating activities).

Operating Activities

Direct Method – Top to bottom

	Collections from customers
+	Interest & dividends received
+	Proceeds from sale of trading securities
+	Other operating cash inflows
−	Payments for merchandise
−	Payments for expense
−	Payments for interest
−	Payments for income taxes
−	Payments to acquire trading securities
−	Other operating cash outflows
=	**Cash flows from operating activities**

Direct Method – Top to bottom

Net income	
Noncash revenues	−
Noncash expenses	+
Gains on sales of investments	−
Losses on sales of investments	+
Gains on sales of plant assets	−
Losses on sales of plant assets	+
Increases in current assets	−
Decreases in current assets	+
Decreases in current liabilities	−
Increases in current liabilities	+
Cash flows from operating activities	**=**

Must be equal

Components of Direct Method

Collections from customers (plug)	xxx	
Increase in accounts receivable (given)	xxx	
Decrease in accounts receivable (given)		xxx
Sales (given)		xxx
Increase in inventory (given)	xxx	
Decrease in accounts payable (given)	xxx	
Cost of sales (given)	xxx	
Decrease in inventory (given)		xxx
Increase in accounts payable (given)		xxx
Payments for merchandise (plug)		xxx

Adjustments Under Indirect Method

- Credit changes are addbacks/debit changes are subtractions, for example
  - Increase in accumulated depreciation added back
  - Increase in accounts payable added back
  - Increase in accounts receivable subtracted
  - Decrease in accounts payable subtracted

Investing Activities

Principal collections on loans receivable

- \+   Proceeds from sale of investments (except trading securities)
- \+   Proceeds from sale of plant assets
- −   Loans made
- −   Payments to acquire investments (except trading securities)
- −   Payments to acquire plant assets
- =   **Cash flows from investing activities**

Financing Activities

Proceeds from borrowings
+   Proceeds from issuing stock
−   Debt principal payments
−   Payments to reacquire stock
−   Payments for dividends
=   **Cash flows from financing activities**

Other Disclosures

With direct method:

Reconciliation of net income to cash flows from operating activities (indirect method)

With indirect method:

Payments for interest
Payments for income taxes

With all cash flow statements:

Schedule of noncash investing and financing activities

IFRS and Cash Flows

- Interest/dividends in either financing or operations sections but must be consistent

BUSINESS COMBINATIONS

Consolidation is required whenever the acquirer has control over another entity.

- Acquirer is the entity that obtains control of one or more businesses in the business combination
- Ownership of majority of voting stock generally indicates control
- Consolidation is required even if control situation is temporary
- Consolidation is not appropriate when a majority shareholder doesn't have effective control:
    - Company is in bankruptcy or reorganization
    - Foreign exchange controls limit power to keep control of subsidiary assets

Business Combinations (continued)

- All consolidations are accounted for as acquisitions
  - The acquirer shall recognize goodwill, the identifiable assets acquired, the liabilities assumed, any noncontrolling interest in the acquiree, and any residual goodwill
  - Recognize separately
    - Acquisition-related costs
    - Assets acquired and liabilities assumed arising from *contractual contingencies*
    - Bargain purchase (fair value of assets acquired > amount paid) recognized as gain
    - Fair values of research and development assets
    - Changes in the value of acquirer deferred tax benefits

Accounting for an Acquisition

Combination – Records combined

Assets (at fair market values)	xxx	
Separately identifiable assets	xx	
Goodwill (plug)	x	
Liabilities (at fair market values)		xxx
Stockholders' equity (2 steps) *		xxx
OR		
Cash (amount paid)		xxx

Combination – Records not combined

Investment (fair value of net assets)   xxx

    Stockholders' equity (same 2 steps)   xxx

OR

    Cash (amount paid)   xxx

* Credit common stock for par value of shares issued and credit APIC for difference between fair value and par value of shares issued

Earnings

Consolidated net income:

Parent's net income
+ Subsidiary's net income from date of acquisition
± Effects of intercompany transactions
− Depreciation on difference between fair value and carrying value of sub's assets
− Impairment losses on goodwill (if applicable)
= Consolidated net income

Retained Earnings – Year of Combination

Beginning retained earnings – Parent's beginning balance
+ Consolidated net income
− Parent's dividends for entire period
= Ending retained earnings

CONSOLIDATIONS

Eliminate the Investment

Example 1 – Date of combination – no goodwill or minority interest

Inventory (excess of fair value over carrying value)	xxx	
Land (excess of fair value over carrying value)	xxx	
Depreciable assets (excess of fair value over carrying value)	xxx	
Common stock (sub's balance)	xxx	
APIC (sub's balance)	xxx	
Retained earnings (sub's balance)	xxx	
Investment		xxx

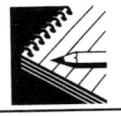

Example 2 – Date of combination – no goodwill with minority interest

Inventory (excess of fair value over carrying value)	xxx
Land (excess of fair value over carrying value)	xxx
Depreciable assets (excess of fair value over carrying value)	xxx
Common stock (sub's balance)	xxx
APIC (sub's balance)	xxx
Retained earnings (sub's balance)	xxx
Minority interest (sub's total stockholders' equity × minority interest percentage)	**xxx**
Investment	xxx

Example 3 – Date of combination – goodwill and minority interest

Inventory (excess of fair value over carrying value)	xxx	
Land (excess of fair value over carrying value)	xxx	
Depreciable assets (excess of fair value over carrying value)	xxx	
Goodwill (plug)	**xxx**	
Common stock (sub's balance)	xxx	
APIC (sub's balance)	xxx	
Retained earnings (sub's balance)	xxx	
Minority interest (sub's total stockholders' equity × minority interest percentage)		xxx
Investment		xxx

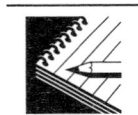

Eliminate the Investment (continued)

Calculating goodwill – 4 steps

1) Determine amount paid for acquisition
2) Compare to book value of sub's underlying net assets
3) Subtract difference between fair values and book values of sub's assets
4) Remainder is goodwill

Additional entries – after date of acquisition

- Debit cost of sales instead of inventory for fair market value adjustment
- Recognize depreciation on excess of fair value over carrying value of depreciable assets
- Recognize impairment of goodwill (if FMV of goodwill is less than carrying amount)

Eliminating Entries

Intercompany Sales of Inventory

Eliminate gross amount of intercompany sales

Sales	xxx	
Cost of sales		xxx

Eliminate intercompany profit included in ending inventory

Cost of sales	xxx	
Inventory		xxx

Eliminate unpaid portion of intercompany sales

Accounts payable	xxx	
Accounts receivable		xxx

Intercompany Sales of Property, Plant, & Equipment

Eliminate intercompany gain or loss

Gain on sale (amount recognized)	xxx	
Depreciable asset		xxx

Adjust depreciation

Accumulated depreciation (amount of gain divided by remaining useful life)	xxx	
Depreciation expense		xxx

Intercompany Bond Holdings

Eliminate intercompany investment in bonds

Bonds payable (face amount of bonds acquired)	xxx		
Bond premium or discount (amount related to intercompany bonds)	xxx	or	xxx
Gain or loss on retirement (plug)	Xxx	or	xxx
Investment in bonds (carrying value)			xxx

Variable Interest Entities (VIE)

Also known as special-purpose entities

Control is achieved based on contractual, ownership, or other pecuniary interests

Primary beneficiary — the entity that has controlling financial interest in the VIE and must consolidate it. This must be reassessed every year.

Both conditions must exist for control:

1. Having the power to direct the significant activities of the VIE, and
2. The entity has the obligation to absorb significant losses of the VIE or the right to receive significant benefits.

Qualitative approach used to determine control when power is shared among unrelated parties, which could lead to none of the entities consolidating the VIE.

Kick-outs rights — the ability to remove the reporting entity who has the power to direct the VIE's significant activities

Participating rights — the ability to block the reporting entity with the power to direct the VIE's significant activities

Push-Down Accounting

The method used to prepare the separate financial statements for significant, very large subsidiaries that are either wholly owned or substantially owned (>90%)

SEC requires (for publicly traded companies) a one-time adjustment under the acquisition method to revalue the subsidiary's assets and liabilities to fair value.

The entry is made directly on the books to the subsidiary.

Has no effect on the presentation of the consolidated financial statements or separate parent financial statements.

The subsidiary's financial statements would be recorded at fair value rather than historical cost.

IFRS Business Combinations

- Focus is on the concept of the power to control, with control being the parent's ability to govern the financial and operating policies of an entity to obtain benefits. Control is presumed to exist if parent owns more than 50% of the votes, and potential voting rights must be considered.
- Special-purpose entities
    - IFRS: Consolidated when the substance of the relationship indicates that an entity controls the SPE
- Consolidated financial statements required except when parent is a wholly owned subsidiary
- Equity method Investments must use equity method (i.e., no fair value option)
- Joint ventures can use either equity method or proportionate consolidation method
- Push-down accounting not allowed

Investments in Derivative Securities

Derivatives – Derive their value from other assets. Examples:

- Stock option – value based on underlying stock price
- Commodity futures contract – value based on underlying commodity price

Initially recorded at cost (or allocated amount) – Reported on balance sheet at fair value

- Trading security – unrealized gains and losses on income statement
- Available for sale security – unrealized gains and losses reported as other comprehensive income in stockholders' equity

Characteristics of Derivatives

Settlement in cash or assets easily convertible to cash (such as marketable securities)

Underlying index on which value of derivative is based (usually the price of some asset)

No or little net investment at time of creation:

- Futures-based derivative involves no payments at all when derivative created

  - Such a derivative must be settled on settlement date in all cases

- Options-based derivative involves small premium payment when derivative created

  - Option holder has right not to settle derivative if results would be unfavorable
  - Payment of premium when derivative created is price of this option

Use of Derivatives

Speculative – Attempt to profit from favorable change in underlying index

- Gain or loss on change in fair value reported in ordinary income

Certain derivatives qualify as hedge instruments and must meet the following criteria:

- Sufficient documentation must be provided at designation
- The hedge must be highly effective throughout its life
  - It must have the ability to generate changes measured every three months (minimum)
  - It must move in the opposite direction to the offsetting item
  - The cumulative change in value of the hedging instrument should be between 80% and 125% of offsetting item
  - The method assessing effectiveness must be consistent with risk management approach
  - Similar hedges should be assessed similarly
- If a hedge is not 100% effective, the ineffective portion must be reported in current earnings

Use of Derivatives (continued)

Fair Value Hedge – Attempt to offset risk of existing asset, liability, or commitment

- Gain or loss on change in derivative reported in ordinary income
  - Should approximately offset loss or gain on item being hedged

Cash Flow Hedge – Attempt to offset risk associated with future expected transactions

- Gain or loss excluded from ordinary income until offsetting future event affects income
  - Reported as part of other comprehensive income until that time

Foreign Currency Hedge – Attempt to offset exposure to foreign currencies

- Gain or loss reported in current earnings or other comprehensive income depending on type of foreign currency hedge (foreign-currency-denominated firm commitment, available-for-sale security, forecasted transaction, net investment in a foreign operation)

Financial Instruments

Risk of loss

Market risk – Losses due to fluctuations in market place

Credit risk – Losses due to nonperformance of other party

Concentration of credit risk – Several instruments have common characteristics resulting in similar risks

Required Disclosures

- Fair value
- Off-balance-sheet credit risk – credit risk that is not already reflected as an accrued contingency
- Concentration of credit risk
- Hedging disclosures

  - Objective and strategies
  - Context to understand instrument
  - Risk management policies
  - A list of hedged instruments

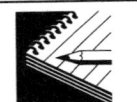

IFRS Derivatives

- No requirement for net settlement
- Embedded derivatives: Cannot reassess if "clearly and closely related" unless change in contract that significantly affects cash flows

Fair Value Option and Measurements

The fair value option

- May be applied instrument by instrument, with a few exceptions, such as investments otherwise accounted for by the equity method
- Is irrevocable
- Is applied only to entire instruments and not to portions of instruments

Available for

- Recognized financial assets and financial liabilities with the following major exceptions:
    - An investment in a subsidiary that the entity is required to consolidate
    - Pension and other postretirement benefit plans including employee stock plans
    - Lease assets and liabilities
    - Deposit liabilities, of banks, savings and loan associations, credit unions, etc.
- Firm commitments that would otherwise not be recognized at inception and that involve only financial instruments

The fair value option (continued)

- Nonfinancial insurance contracts and warranties that the insurer can settle by paying a third party to provide those goods or services
- Host financial instruments resulting from separation of an embedded nonfinancial derivative instrument from a nonfinancial hybrid instrument

Recognize unrealized gains and losses in earnings for businesses and in statement of activities for nonprofit organizations.

Fair Value defined

- Exchange price

    - Orderly transaction between market participants to sell the asset or transfer the liability in the principal or most advantageous market for the asset or liability under current market conditions
    - Value is a market-based measurement, not an entity-specific measurement
    - Includes assumptions about

        - Risk inherent in a particular valuation technique or inputs to the valuation technique
        - Effect of a restriction on the sale or use of an asset
        - Nonperformance risk

Expanded disclosures on the inputs used to measure fair value

Fair Value defined (continued)

Level 1

- Quoted prices in active markets for identical assets or liabilities

Level 2

- Inputs such as quoted prices on similar assets or liabilities or observable for the asset or liability such as interest rates and yield curves

Level 3

- Unobservable inputs for the asset or liability that reflect the reporting entity's own assumptions about the assumptions that market participants would use in pricing the asset or liability (including assumptions about risk).

SEGMENT REPORTING

Definition of Segments

Segments identified using management approach:

- Component earns revenue and incurs expenses
- Separate information is available
- Component is evaluated regularly by top management

Reportable Segments - 3 Tests

Revenue test – Segment revenues ≥ 10% of total revenues

Asset test – Segment identifiable assets ≥ 10% of total assets

Profit or loss test

- Combine profits for all profitable segments
- Combine losses for all losing segments
- Select larger amount
- Segments profit or loss ≥ 10% of larger amount

Disclosures for Reportable Segments

Segment profit or loss

- Segment revenues include intersegment sales
- Deduct traceable operating expenses and allocated indirect operating expenses
- Do not deduct general corporate expenses

Segment revenues

Segment assets

Interest revenue & expense

Depreciation, depletion, & amortization

Other items

PARTNERSHIP

Admitting a Partner

Calculating the Contribution – No Goodwill or Bonus

    Partnership equity (before new partner's contribution)

    ÷   100% – new partner's percentage

    =   Total capital after contribution

    ×   New partner's percentage

    =   Amount to be contributed

Journal entry:

Cash	xxx	
New partner's equity		xxx

Excess Contribution by New Partner – Bonus Method

Partnership equity (before new partner's contribution)

+ New partner's contribution   New partner's contribution

= Total capital after contribution

× New partner's percentage

= New partner's capital   − New partner's capital

                                   = Bonus to existing partners

Journal entry:

Cash (new partner's contribution)	xxx	
Capital, new partner (amount calculated)		xxx
Capital, existing partners (bonus amount)		xxx

Bonus is allocated to existing partners using their P & L percentages

---

Excess Contribution by New Partner – Goodwill Method

New partner's contribution

÷　New partner's percentage

=　Total capital after contribution

−　Total capital of partnership (existing capital + contribution)

=　Goodwill to existing partners

Journal entry:

Cash (new partner's contribution)	xxx	
Capital, new partner (new partner's contribution)		xxx
Goodwill (amount calculated)	xxx	
Capital, existing partners		xxx

Goodwill is allocated to existing partners using their P & L percentages

Contribution Below New Partner's Capital – Bonus Method

Partnership equity (before new partner's contribution)
+   New partner's contribution
=   Total capital after contribution
×   New partner's percentage
=   New partner's capital
−   New partner's contribution
=   Bonus to new partner

Journal entry:

Cash (new partner's contribution)	xxx	
Capital, existing partners (bonus amount)	xxx	
Capital, new partner (amount calculated)		xxx

Bonus is allocated to existing partners using their P & L percentages

---

Contribution Below New Partner's Capital – Goodwill Method

Partnership equity (before new partner's contribution)

÷   100% - new partner's percentage

=   Total capital after contribution

×   New partner's percentage

=   New partner's capital

−   New partner's contribution

=   Goodwill

Journal entry:

Cash (new partner's contribution)	xxx	
Goodwill (amount calculated)	xxx	
Capital, new partner (total)		xxx

Retiring a Partner

Payment Exceeds Partner's Balance – Bonus Method

Capital, retiring partner (existing balance)	xxx	
Capital, remaining partners (difference – bonus)	xxx	
Cash (amount paid)		xxx

Bonus to new partner is allocated to existing partners using their P & L percentages

Payment Exceeds Partner's Balance – Goodwill Method

Amount paid to retiring partner

÷   Retiring partner's percentage

=   Value of partnership on date of retirement

−   Partnership equity before retirement

=   Goodwill

Journal entries:

Goodwill (amount calculated)	xxx	
Capital, all partners		xxx

Goodwill is allocated according to the partners' P & L percentages

Capital, retiring partner	xxx	
Cash (amount paid to retiring partner)		xxx

Partnership Liquidation – 5 steps

1) Combine each partner's capital account with loans to or from that partner
2) Allocate gain or loss on assets sold to partners
3) Assume remaining assets are total loss – allocate to partners
4) Eliminate any partner's negative balance by allocating to remaining partners using their P & L percentages
5) Resulting balances will be amounts to be distributed to remaining partners

FOREIGN CURRENCY

Foreign Currency Transactions

Receivable or payable

- Record at **spot rate**
- Adjust to new spot rate on each financial statement date

Journal entry:

Receivable or payable	xxx	
Foreign currency transaction gain		xxx
OR		
Foreign currency transaction loss	xxx	
Receivable or payable		xxx

Gain or loss = Change in spot rate × Receivable or payable (in foreign currency)

Forward Exchange Contracts

All gains and losses measured using forward rate – rate expected to be in effect when settled

Hedge – Protection against change in exchange rate related to **existing** receivable or payable

- Change in forward rate results in gain or loss on hedge
- This will approximately offset loss or gain on change in spot rate on receivable or payable

Special hedge contracts:

- Hedge of foreign currency investment – gains or losses reported in equity – excluded from net income but included in comprehensive income
- Hedge of foreign commitment – gain or loss deferred and offset against transaction

Speculative contracts – Entered into in anticipation of change in rate

- Change in forward rate results in gain or loss

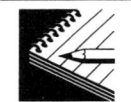

Foreign Currency Financial Statements

Conversion to U.S. $:

Local currency ⟶ Functional currency ⟶ Reporting currency (US $)

Remeasurement   Translation

Functional Currency – Currency of primary economic environment in which entity operates.

1) Functional currency = local currency

- Translate from local currency to U.S. $

2) Functional currency = U.S. $

- Remeasure from local currency to U.S. $

3) Functional currency neither local currency nor U.S. $

- Remeasure from local currency to functional currency
- Translate from functional currency to U.S. $

Remeasurement and Translation

Remeasurement	**Translation**
Historical rate:	Rate at balance sheet date:*
Nonmonetary assets and liabilities	Assets and liabilities
Contributed capital accounts	Rate in effect on transaction date
Revenue and expense accounts	(or weighted-average rate for period):
Current rate:	Revenues and expenses
All other items	Gains and losses
Difference:	Difference:
Remeasurement gain or loss	Translation gain or loss
Reported on income statement	Component of stockholders' equity
	Excluded from net income
	Included in comprehensive income

* *NOTE: To prepare a translated Statement of Cash Flows, the assets and liabilities must be translated at the weighted-average rate, not the rate at the balance sheet date.*

INTERIM FINANCIAL STATEMENTS

General Rules

1) Revenues & expenses recognized in interim period earned or incurred
2) Same principles as applied to annual financial statements

Special Rules

Inventory Losses

Expected to recover within annual period

- Not recognized in interim period
- Offset against recovery in subsequent interim period
- Recognized when clear that recovery will not occur

Not expected to recover within annual period

- Recognized in interim period
- Recovery in subsequent interim period recognized

Income Taxes

Estimate of rate that applies to annual period

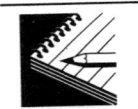

Other Items

Property taxes – allocated among interim periods

Repairs & maintenance

- Generally recognized in interim period when incurred (including major repairs)
- Allocated to current & subsequent interim periods when future benefit results

Disposal of a segment – recognized in interim period in which it occurs

Extraordinary item – recognized in interim period in which it occurs

IFRS: Interim

- Discrete report, therefore use same accounting policies as in year-end financial statements
- Not required

PERSONAL FINANCIAL STATEMENTS

Basic Statements

Statement of Financial Condition

Statement of Changes in Net Worth

Principles Applied

Assets & liabilities – Reported at fair market values

Business interests – Reported as single amount

Real estate

- When operated as business – reported net of mortgage
- When not operated as business – asset and mortgage reported separately

Retirement plans

- Contributions & earnings on contributions by employee included
- Contributions & earnings on contributions by employer included to extent vested

Principles Applied (continued)

Life insurance – Cash surrender value minus borrowings against policy

Income taxes – 2 components

- Income taxes on individual's income for year to date
- Tax effect on difference between tax basis and fair values of assets and liabilities

Other liabilities

- Current payoff amount, if available
- Otherwise, present value of future payments

GOVERNMENTAL (STATE AND LOCAL) ACCOUNTING

GASB Concept Statements set forth fundamentals on which governmental accounting and reporting standards will be based

Objective of governmental accounting & reporting – **accountability**

- Provide useful information
- Benefit wide range of users

Concepts Statement No. 1 identified three primary users of the external state and local governmental financial reports

- The citizenry
- Legislative and oversight bodies
- Investors and creditors

GOVERNMENTAL (STATE AND LOCAL) ACCOUNTING (CONTINUED)

Governmental financial information should:

- Demonstrate operations within legal restraints imposed by citizens
- Communicate compliance with laws & regulations related to raising & spending money
- Demonstrate **interperiod equity** – current period expenditures financed with current revenues

To demonstrate full accountability for all activities, information must include:

- Cost of services
- Sufficiency of revenues for services provided
- Financial position

The concepts statements encourage Service Efforts and Accomplishment (SEA) reporting

- SEA reporting provides more complete information about a governmental entity's performance than can be provided by traditional financial statements and schedules

Funds

Government comprised of funds – self-balancing sets of accounts – 3 categories

- Governmental
- Proprietary
- Fiduciary

Methods of Accounting

Funds of a governmental unit use two methods of accounting

- Most funds use **modified accrual accounting**
- Some funds use accrual accounting

Modified Accrual Accounting

Differs from accrual accounting:

- Focus of financial reporting is financial position & flow of resources
- Revenues are recognized when they become available & measurable
- Expenditures are recorded when goods or services are obtained
- Expenditures classified by **object, function, or character**

Financial Statements of Governmental Units

General purpose financial statements – referred to as **Comprehensive Annual Financial Report (CAFR)** – 5 components

- Management discussions & analysis – Presented before financial statements
- Government-wide financial statements
- Fund financial statements
- Notes to financial statements
- Required supplementary information – Presented after financial statements and notes

A **component unit** is a legally separate organization for which the elected officials of a primary government are financially accountable.

Financial Statements of Governmental Units (continued)

Users should be able to distinguish between primary government & component units – component units may be **blended** when either:

- Governing body of component is essentially the same as that of the primary government
- The component provides services almost exclusively for the primary government
- The component unit's total debt outstanding, including leases, is expected to be repaid entirely or almost entirely by the primary government

Most component units will be **discretely presented**

Management Discussion & Analysis (MD&A)

Introduces basic financial statements & provides analytical overview of government's financial activities

Should include:

- Condensed comparison of current year financial information to prior year
- Analysis of overall financial position and results of operations
- Analysis of balances and transactions in individual funds
- Analysis of significant budget variances
- Description of capital assets and long-term debt activity during the period
- Currently known facts, decisions, or conditions expected to affect financial position or results of operations

Government-Wide Financial Statements

Consist of:

- Statement of Net Position
- Statement of Activities

Report on overall government

- Do not display information about individual funds
- Exclude fiduciary activities or component units that are fiduciary
- Distinction made between primary government and discretely presented component units
- Distinction made between government-type activities and business-type activities of primary government
- Government-type activities include governmental funds & internal service funds
- Business-type activities include enterprise funds only

Characteristics of Government-Wide Financial Statements

Use economic measurement focus for all assets, liabilities, revenues, expenses, gains, & losses

Apply accrual basis of accounting

Revenues from exchanges or exchange-like transactions recognized in period of exchange

Revenues from nonexchange transactions:

- **Derived tax revenues** imposed on exchange transactions recognized as asset & revenues when exchange occurs
- **Imposed nonexchange revenues** imposed on nongovernment agencies recognized as asset when government has enforceable claim & as revenues when use of resources required or permitted
- **Government-mandated nonexchange transactions** provided by one level of government for another recognized as asset & revenue (or liability & expense) when all eligibility requirements met
- **Voluntary nonexchange transactions** recognized similarly to government-mandated nonexchange transactions

Statement of Net Position

Presents assets, liabilities, deferred outflows of resources, and deferred inflows of resources

- Assets & liabilities in order of liquidity
- Current & noncurrent portions of liabilities reported
- Assets + Deferred Outflows of Resources – Liabilities – Deferred Inflows of Resources = Net Position

3 categories of net position

- **Net assets invested in capital assets, net of related debt** – All capital assets, including restricted assets, net of depreciation & reduced by related debt
- **Restricted net position** – Items with externally imposed restrictions on use distinguishing major categories of restrictions
- **Unrestricted net position** – Remainder

Format of Statement of Net Position

Assets, deferred outflows of resources, liabilities, deferred inflows of resources & net position reported for primary government

- Separate columns for government-type activities & business-type activities
- Amounts combined in total column

Assets, deferred outflows of resources, liabilities, deferred inflows of resources & net position also reported for component units

- Amounts reported similarly as those for primary government
- Column is **not** combined with totals for primary government

Statement of Activities

Self-financing activities distinguished from those drawing from general revenues

For each government function

- Net expense or revenue
- Relative burden

Governmental activities presented by function

Business-type activities presented by business segment

Items reported separately after net expenses of government's functions:

- General revenues
- Contributions to term & permanent endowments
- Contributions to permanent fund principal
- Special items – those that are unusual **or** infrequent
- Extraordinary items – those that are unusual **and** infrequent
- Transfers

Items on Statement of Activities

Depreciation – indirect expense charged to function with asset

- Allocated among functions for shared assets
- Not required to be allocated to functions for general capital assets
- Not allocated to functions for eligible general infrastructure assets

  - Government uses an asset management system
  - Government documents assets preserved appropriately

Revenues classified into categories

- Amounts received from users or beneficiaries of a program always **program revenues**
- Amounts received from parties outside citizenry are **general revenues** if unrestricted or program revenues if restricted to specific programs
- Amounts received from taxpayers always general revenues
- Amounts generated by the government usually general revenues
- Contributions to term & permanent endowments, contributions to permanent fund principal, special & extraordinary items, & transfers reported separately

Format of Statement of Activities

Information for each program or function reported separately:

- Expenses
- Charges for services
- Operating grants & contributions
- Capital grants & contributions

Difference between expenses & revenues reported for each program

- Equal to change in net position
- Separated into columns for governmental activities and business-type activities
- Combined into a total column

Remaining items (general revenues, grants & contributions, special & extraordinary items, & transfers) reported separately below functions & programs

- Divided into governmental activities & business-type activities with total column
- Provides change in net position & ending net position with same amounts as Statement of Net Position
- Separate column for component units not combined into total

Additional Characteristics of Government-Wide Financial Statements

Internal Amounts

- Eliminated to avoid doubling up
- Interfund receivables & payables eliminated
- Amounts due between government-type & business-type activities presented as offsetting internal balances

Capital assets include the following:

- Land, land improvements, & easements
- Buildings & building improvements
- Vehicles, machinery, & equipment
- Works of art & historical treasures
- Infrastructure

Additional Characteristics of Government-Wide Financial Statements (continued)

- All other tangible & intangible assets with initial useful lives > a single period
    - Only identifiable intangibles
    - Internally generated intangibles begin to be capitalized if
        - Objective and capacity identified
        - Feasible
        - Intent to complete
- Pension plans
    - **Single-employer defined benefit plan** or **agent defined benefit plan**
        - Reports a net pension liability, which is measured as the portion of the actuarial present value of projected benefit payments attributable to past periods of employee service minus the pension plan's fiduciary net position

Accounting for Capital Assets & Infrastructure

Capital assets reported at historical cost

- Includes capitalized interest & costs of getting asset ready for intended use
- Depreciated over useful lives
- Inexhaustible assets not depreciated
- Infrastructure assets may be depreciated under modified approach

Infrastructure includes:

- Capital assets with longer lives than most capital assets that are normally stationary
- Roads, bridges, tunnels, drainage systems, water & sewer systems, dams, & lighting systems

Eligible infrastructure assets not depreciated

- Must be part of network or subsystem maintained & preserved at established condition levels
- Additions & improvements increasing capacity or efficiency capitalized
- Other expenditures expensed

Fund Financial Statements

Governmental funds include:

- General fund
- Special revenue funds
- Capital projects funds
- Debt service funds
- Permanent funds

Proprietary funds include:

- Enterprise funds
- Internal service funds

Fiduciary funds include:

- Pension & other employee benefit trust funds
- Investment trust funds
- Private purpose trust funds
- Agency funds

Financial Statements of Governmental Funds

Statements of governmental funds

- Balance sheet
- Statement of revenues, expenditures, and changes in fund balances

Focus is to report sources, uses, & balances of current financial resources

- Apply modified accrual accounting
- Capital assets & long-term debt not reported as assets or liabilities

Reports include separate columns for each major governmental fund and single column for total of all nonmajor funds:

- General fund is always major
- Others major if assets, liabilities, revenues, expenditures meet the 5% and 10% tests:

  - Fund at least 5% of "total" column in government-wide financial statements
  - Fund at least 10% of "government-type" column in government-wide financial statements.

Balance Sheet

Reports assets, liabilities, & fund balances

- Reported separately for each major governmental fund
- Fund balances segregated into reserved & unreserved

Total fund balances reconciled to net position of governmental activities in government-wide financial statements

Statement of Revenues, Expenditures, & Changes in Fund Balances

Reports inflows, outflows, and balances of current financial resources

- Reported separately for each major governmental fund
- Revenues classified by major source
- Expenditures classified by function

Statement of Revenues, Expenditures, & Changes in Fund Balances (continued)

Format of statement:

Revenues
– Expenditures
= Excess (deficiency) of revenues over expenditures
± Other financing sources and uses
± Special and extraordinary items
= Net change in fund balances
+ Fund balances – beginning of period
= Fund balances – end of period

Change in fund balances reconciled to change in net position of governmental activities in government-wide financial statements

Financial Statements of Proprietary Funds

Statements of proprietary funds

- Statement of net position
- Statement of Revenues, Expenses, and Changes in Fund Net Position
- Statement of Cash Flows

Preparation of statements

- Emphasis is measurement of economic resources
- Prepared under accrual basis of accounting
- Reports include separate column for each enterprise fund meeting 5% and 10% tests:

  - Fund at least 5% of "total" column in government-wide financial statements
  - Fund at least 10% of "business-type" column in government-wide financial statements.
  - Total of nonmajor enterprise funds in a single column
  - Total of all internal service funds in a single column

Financial Statements of Proprietary Funds (continued)

- Four categories
    - Operating
    - Noncapital financing
    - Capital financing
    - Investing
- Derivatives: Reported at fair value
- Evaluated for effectiveness each financial reporting period
- Land held for investment reported at fair value

Statement of Net Position

Prepared in classified format

- Current & noncurrent assets & liabilities distinguished
- Net position reported in same categories as used in government-wide financial statements

Statement of Revenues, Expenses, & Changes in Fund Net Position

Amounts should be the same as net position & changes in net position shown for business-type activities in government-wide financial statements

- Revenues reported by major source
- Operating & nonoperating revenues & expenses distinguished
- Nonoperating revenues & expenses reported after operating income

Statement of Revenues, Expenses, & Changes in Fund Net Position (continued)

Format of statement of revenues, expenses, & changes in fund net position

    Operating revenues (listed by source)

    –   <u>Operating expenses (listed by category)</u>

    =   Operating income or loss

    ±   <u>Nonoperating revenues & expenses</u>

    =   Income before other revenues, expenses, gains, losses, & transfers

    ±   Capital contributions, additions to permanent & term endowments, special & <u>extraordinary items, & transfers</u>

    =   Increase or decrease in net position

    +   <u>Net position – beginning of period</u>

    =   <u>Net position – end of period</u>

Statement of Cash Flows

Shows sources & uses of cash by major classification

- Operating activities reported using direct method
- Noncapital financing activities
- Capital & related financing activities
- Investing activities

Operating income reconciled to cash flows from operating activities (indirect method)

Financial Statements of Fiduciary Funds

Statements of fiduciary funds

- Statement of Net Position
- Statement of Changes in Fiduciary Net Position

Focus of fiduciary financial statements

- Emphasis on measurement of economic resources
- Prepared using accrual basis of accounting

Report includes separate column for each major fiduciary fund and column for total of all non-major fiduciary funds.

- Selection of major funds based on judgment of entity management
- No 5% and 10% tests since fiduciary funds weren't included in government-wide financial statements

Notes to Government Financial Statements

Intended to provide information needed for fair presentation of financial statements

Notes will include:

- Summary of significant accounting policies
- Disclosure about capital assets & long-term liabilities
- Disclosure about major classes of capital assets
- Disclosure about donor-restricted endowments
- Segment information

Required Supplementary Information

Presented in addition to MD & A

Consists of:

- Schedule of Funding Progress for all Pension Trust Funds
- Schedule of Employer Contributions to all Pension Trust Funds
- Budgetary comparison schedules for governmental funds (reporting basis is same as that chosen by legislative body for budget, and not necessarily that used for financial statements)
- Information about infrastructure reported under the modified approach
- Claims development information for any public entity risk pools

Governmental Funds

A governmental unit maintains 5 types of governmental funds

- General fund – all activities not accounted for in another fund

  - Only fund that reports positive unassigned fund balance

Governmental Funds (continued)

- Special revenue funds – account for revenues earmarked to finance specific activities
- Capital projects funds – account for construction of fixed assets
- Debt service fund – accumulates resources for payment of general obligation debts of other governmental funds
- Permanent funds – account for resources that are legally restricted
- Fixed assets and LT debt not reported in governmental funds
- Instead, reported in government-wide financial statements
- Four fund balance classifications

  - Nonspendable (either in form, e.g., inventory, or legally)
  - Restricted (either by contributor or law)
  - Committed to specific purposes (by highest level of governmental decision-making authority)
  - Assigned (intend to spend for purpose but not bound to
  - Unassigned (residual of general fund)

General Fund Accounting

A governmental unit will have one general fund

- Annual budget is recorded at the beginning of the year
- Revenues, expenditure, & other financing sources & uses are recorded during the year
- Adjustments are made at the balance sheet date
- Budgetary accounts are closed at year-end

Beginning of Year

Governmental unit adopts annual budget for general fund

Budget recorded with following entry:

Estimated revenues control	xxx			
Estimated other financing sources	xxx			
Budgetary fund balance	xxx	or	xxx	
Appropriations			xxx	
Estimated other financing uses			xxx	

Estimated revenues control = revenues expected to be collected during the year

Estimated other financing sources = estimate of proceeds from bond issues & operating transfers in

Budgetary fund balance = plug – amount required to balance the entry

Appropriations = expenditures expected during the year

Estimated other financing uses = expected operating transfers out

---

During the Year

Revenue cycle consists of billing certain revenues, such as property taxes, collecting billed revenues, writing off uncollectible billings, & collecting unbilled revenues

Billing of revenues:

Taxes receivable	xxx	
Allowance for estimated uncollectible taxes		xxx
Deferred revenues		xxx
Revenues control		xxx

Taxes receivable = amount billed

Allowance for estimated uncollectible taxes = billings expected to be uncollectible

- This amount may be adjusted upward or downward during the year
- Offsetting entry will be to revenues control

Deferred revenues = portion of billed taxes expected to be collected more than 60 days after close of current year

During the Year (continued)

Revenues control = portion of billed taxes expected to be collected during the current year or within 60 days of close

Collecting billed revenues:

Cash	xxx	
Taxes receivable		xxx

Writing off uncollectible amounts:

Allowance for estimated uncollectible taxes	xxx	
Taxes receivable		xxx

Collecting unbilled revenues:

Cash	xxx	
Revenues control		xxx

During the Year (continued)

Spending cycle consists of ordering goods & services, receiving the goods & services, and paying for them

Ordering goods & services:

Encumbrances control (estimated cost)	xxx	
Budgetary fund balance reserved for encumbrances		xxx

Receiving goods & services:

Budgetary fund balance reserved for encumbrances (estimated cost)	xxx	
Encumbrances control		xxx
Expenditures control (actual cost)	xxx	
Vouchers payable		xxx

During the Year (continued)

Payment:

Vouchers payable	xxx	
Cash		xxx

Other financing sources & uses are recorded as the transactions occur:

- Proceeds of long-term debit issues are recorded as other financing sources when received
- Operating transfers to or from other funds are reported as other financing uses or sources as the funds are transferred

Adjustments at Balance Sheet Date

Closing entry – eliminating revenues, expenditures, & encumbrances:

Revenues control	xxx	
Unreserved fund balance (plug)	xxx or	xxx
Expenditures control		xxx
Encumbrances control		xxx

The remaining balance in the budgetary fund balance reserved for encumbrances is transferred to a nonbudgetary account:

Budgetary fund balance reserved for encumbrances	xxx	
Fund balance reserved for encumbrances		xxx

Adjustments at Balance Sheet Date (continued)

The governmental unit may decide to recognize inventory as an asset:

Inventories (increase)	xxx	
Fund balance reserved for inventories		xxx

or

Fund balance reserved for inventories	xxx	
Inventories (decrease)		xxx

End of Year

Budget recorded in beginning of year is reversed:

Appropriations	xxx	
Estimated other financing uses	xxx	
Budgetary fund balance	xxx or	xxx
Estimated revenues control		xxx
Estimated other financing sources		xxx

Special Revenue Fund

Used to account for revenues that must be used for a particular purpose

- Accounting identical to general fund

Capital Projects Fund

Used to account for construction of fixed assets

- Fund opened when project commences & closed when project complete
- Accounting similar to general fund

Differences in accounting for capital projects fund:

1) Budgetary entries generally not made
2) Expenditures generally made under contract

- Credit contracts payable
- Credit retention payable for deferred payments

Debt Service Fund

Used to account for funds accumulated to make principal & interest payments on general obligation debts

- Expenditures include principal & interest payable in current period
- Resources consist of amounts transferred from other funds (other financing sources) & earnings on investments (revenues)

Amounts used for interest payments separated from amounts used for principal payments

Cash for interest	xxx	
Cash for principal	xxx	
Other financing sources		xxx

Proprietary Funds

Account for governmental activities conducted similarly to business enterprises

Enterprise fund:

- Used to account for business-type activities
- Uses accrual basis accounting
- Earned income recognized as operating revenues
- Shared taxes reported as nonoperating revenues

Internal service fund:

- Used to account for services provided to other governmental departments on a fee or cost-reimbursement basis
- Resources come from billings to other funds
- Reported as operating revenues

Fiduciary Funds

Pension Trust Fund

Accounts for contributions made by government & employees using accrual accounting

Additional information in notes and supplementary information following notes will include:

- Descriptive information about the plan
- Information about plan investments
- Information about the terms of receivables and nature of reserves
- Components of the pension liability
- Significant assumptions to measure the pension liability
- The measurement date
- A ten-year schedule of changes in pension liability
- A ten-year schedule of the amounts of total pension liability, fiduciary net position, net pension liability, the covered-employee payroll, and selected ratios
- A ten-year schedule of the actuarial computed required contribution, the required contribution, the actual contribution to the plan, and selected ratios
- A ten-year schedule of the annual money-weighted return on pension plan assets

Investment Trust Fund

Accounts for assets received from other governments units to be invested on their behalf.

- Uses accrual accounting

Private Purpose Trust Fund

Accounts for resources held on behalf of private persons or organizations.

- Uses accrual accounting

Agency Fund

Accounts for money collected for various funds, other governments, or outsiders

- Includes only balance sheet accounts
- Assets always equal liabilities
- Uses modified accrual accounting

Interfund Transactions

Nonreciprocal transfers are transfers of resources from one fund to another without any receipts of goods or services, such as a transfer of money from the general fund to a capital projects fund.

Paying fund:

Other financing uses control	xxx	
Cash		xxx

Receiving fund:

Cash	xxx	
Other financing uses control		xxx

Interfund Transactions (continued)

Reciprocal transfers occur when one fund acquires goods or services from another in a transaction similar to one that would occur with outsiders.

Paying fund:

Expenditures control **or** Expenses	xxx	
Cash		xxx

Receiving fund:

Cash	xxx	
Revenues control		xxx

Reimbursements occur when one fund makes payments on behalf of another fund

Reimbursing fund:

Expenditures control **or** Expenses	xxx	
Cash		xxx

Interfund Transactions (continued)

Receiving fund:

    Cash   xxx

        Expenditures control **or** Expenses   xxx

Loans may be made from one fund to another

Lending fund:

    Due from other fund (fund identified)   xxx

        Cash   xxx

Receiving fund:

    Cash   xxx

        Due from other fund (fund identified)   xxx

Solid Waste Landfill Operations

Environmental Protection Agency imposes requirements on solid waste landfills

- Procedures for closures
- Procedures for postclosure care

Procedures represent long-term obligations accounted for as long-term debt

- Costs to be incurred by governmental funds accounted for in general long-term debt account group
- Expenditures in governmental funds reduce general long-term debt account group balances
- Costs to be incurred by proprietary funds accounted for directly in funds
- Costs associated with closure and postclosure procedures accounted for during periods of operation

ACCOUNTING FOR NONPROFIT ENTITIES

Financial Statements of Not-for-Profit Organizations

All not-for-profit organizations must prepare at least 3 financial statements

Not-for-profit organizations include:

- Hospitals
- Colleges & universities
- Voluntary health & welfare organizations (VHW)

Required financial statements for all types include:

- Statement of Financial Position
- Statement of Activities
- Statement of Cash Flows

VHWs must also prepare a Statement of Functional Expenses

Statement of Financial Position

Includes assets, liabilities, & net assets

- Unrestricted net assets – available for general use, including those set aside by board of trustees
- Temporarily restricted net assets – donated by outside party & restricted to specific purpose
- Permanently restricted net assets – donated by outside party & required to be invested with earnings restricted or unrestricted

Statement of Financial Position (continued)

NOT-FOR-PROFIT COMPANY
STATEMENT OF FINANCIAL POSITION
DECEMBER 31, 20X2

Assets:		Liabilities:	
Cash	100	Accounts payable	50
Marketable securities	300	Notes payable	100
Accounts receivable, net	40	Bonds payable	100
Inventory	120	Total liabilities	250
P, P, & E	80	**Net assets:**	
Total assets	640	Unrestricted	45
		Temporarily restricted	305
		Permanently restricted	40
		Total net assets	390
		Total liabilities & net assets	640

Statement of Activities for NPO

Similar to income statement

- Reports revenues, gains, expenses, & losses
- Also reports temporarily restricted assets released from restriction
- Categorized activities among unrestricted, temporarily restricted, & permanently restricted to provide change in net assets for each
- Change added to beginning balance to provide ending net assets for each category

Expenses classified by:

- Object – nature of item or service obtained
- Function – program or activity to which attributed
- Character – period or periods benefited from payments

Statement of Activities (continued)

Not-for-Profit Company
Statement of Activities
For Year Ended December 31, 20X2

	Total	Unrestricted	Temporarily Restricted	Permanently Restricted
Revenues & gains				
Donations	665	265	360	40
Investment income	10	10		
Total revenues & gains	675	275	360	40
Net assets released from restriction				
Research restrictions		100	(100)	
Time restrictions				
Property restrictions		20	(20)	
Total net assets released from restriction		120	(120)	
Expenses & losses				
Depreciation	(10)	(10)		
Program expenses	(190)	(190)		
General & administrative	(85)	(85)		
Salaries	(70)	(70)		
Total expenses & losses	(355)	(355)		
Change in net assets	320	40	240	40
Net assets at December 31, 20X1	70	5	65	
Net assets at December 31, 20X2	390	45	305	40

Statement of Cash Flows for NPO

Similar to statement of cash flows under GAAP

- Special treatment for donated assets restricted for long-term purposes
- Classified as cash flows from financing activities

Statement of Functional Expenses

Classifies expenses into program services & support services

- Program services – expenses directly related to organization's purpose
- Support services – expenses necessary, but not directly related to organization's purpose such as fund-raising & administrative expenses

Expenses classified by (similar to statement of activities):

- Object
- Nature
- Character

Contributions Made to and Received by Not-for-Profit Organizations

In general, contributions are income to a not-for-profit organization

- Those that are part of the major, ongoing, & central operations are revenues
- Those that are not are gains

Unrestricted cash donations:

Cash	xxx	
Donations (unrestricted funds)		xxx

Permanently restricted donations:

Cash	xxx	
Donations (permanently restricted funds)		xxx

Donated services:

Program expense (fair market value)	xxx	
Donations (unrestricted funds)		xxx

Contributions Made to and Received by Not-for-Profit Organizations (continued)

Cash donations restricted for a specific purposes:

When made:

Cash	xxx	
Donations (temporarily restricted funds)		xxx

When used:

Temporarily restricted net assets	xxx	
Unrestricted net assets		xxx
Expense	xxx	
Cash		xxx

Contributions Made to and Received by Not-for-Profit Organizations (continued)

Cash donated for purchase of property:

When made:

Cash	xxx	
Donations (temporarily restricted funds)		xxx

When used:

Temporarily restricted net assets	xxx	
Unrestricted net assets		xxx
Property	xxx	
Cash		xxx

Pledges

Promises by outside parties to donate assets

- Recognized in period of pledge
- Allowance for uncollectible amount established
- Some or all may have time restriction – temporarily restricted
- Some or all may be unrestricted

Pledges	xxx	
Allowance for uncollectible pledges		xxx
Donations (unrestricted funds)		xxx
Donations (temporarily restricted funds)		xxx

Other Donations

Donations of art, antiques, or artifacts not recognized if:

- Asset held for research or exhibition
- Asset preserved & unaltered
- Proceeds from sale of asset to be used to buy additional art, antiques, & artifacts

Donated assets to be held in trust

- Not recognized by not-for-profit organization
- Disclosed in footnotes to financial statements

Hospital Revenues

Patient service revenue recorded at gross value of services

- Billing may be less due to Medicare allowance or employee discount
- Difference recorded in allowance account
- Statement of activities will report net amount

Services provided for free due to charity not recognized as revenues

Special transactions:

- Bad debts recognized as expense on statement of activities, not reduction of revenues
- Miscellaneous revenues from cafeteria, gift shop, parking lot fees, & educational programs classified as other revenue
- Donated supplies reported as operating revenue & expense when used
- Donations of essential services and unrestricted donations are nonoperating revenues

College Tuition Revenues

Students may receive refunds or price breaks

Refunds to students reduce tuition revenues

Price breaks may result from scholarships or reductions for family members of faculty or staff

- Tuition recognized at gross amount
- Price break recognized as expense

Accounting for a Purchase, 209
Accounting for Changing Prices, 30
Accounting for Income Taxes, 152
Accounting for Nonprofit Entities, 301
Accounts Payable, 103
Accounts Receivable, 88
Admitting a Partner, 235
Agency Fund, 296
Applying LIFO, 41
Balance Sheet, 10
Bank Reconciliation, 87
Bankruptcy, 145
Basic EPS, 183
Basic Rules & Concepts, 6
Bond Issue Costs, 136
Bond Retirement, 137
Bonds, 130
Book Value Per Share, 179
Business Combinations, 207, 208
Capital Leases, 118

Capital Projects Fund, 292
Capitalization of Interest, 63
Change in Accounting Principle, 23
Change in Estimate, 25
Characteristics of Derivatives, 222
College Tuition Revenues, 313
Common Stock Subscribed, 162
Compensated Absences, 114
Completed Contract, 60
Computing Net Income, 17
Consolidations, 212
Contingencies, 104, 105
Contributions Made to and Received by Not-for-
    Profit Organizations, 307
Conventional Retail (Lower of Cost or Market),
    55
Convertible Bonds, 138
Converting from Cash Basis to Accrual Basis, 8
Cost of Goods Sold, 38
Cost Recovery Method, 7

Costs Incurred After Acquisition, 64
Coupons, 112
Current Assets & Liabilities, 12, 13
Current Income Tax, 153
Debt Service Fund, 293
Deferred Income Tax Expense or Benefit, 157
Deferred Tax Assets & Liabilities, 156
Depreciation and Depletion, 65
Detachable Warrants, 139
Diluted EPS, 184
Disclosure of Information About Capital
  Structure, 180
Discontinued Operations, 27
Disposal of Property, Plant, & Equipment, 71
Dividends, 167
Dollar Value LIFO, 46
Earnings Per Share, 182
Elements of Financial Statements, 4
Eliminate the Investment, 212, 215
Eliminating Entries, 216
Enterprise fund, 294

Equity Instruments with Characteristics of
  Liabilities, 166
Equity Method, 188
Error Corrections, 26
Errors Affecting Income, 19
Estimated & Accrued Amounts, 106
Extraordinary Items, 21
Fin 48, 159, 160
Financial Instruments, 225
Financial Statement Analysis, 99
Financial Statements of Fiduciary Funds, 280
Financial Statements of Governmental Funds,
  272
Financial Statements of Governmental Units,
  258, 259
Financial Statements of Not-for-Profit
  Organizations, 301
Financial Statements of Proprietary Funds, 275,
  276
Financing Activities, 205
Financing Receivables - Discounting, 95

Foreign Currency, 243
Foreign Currency Financial Statements, 245
Foreign Currency Transactions, 243
Forward Exchange Contracts, 244
Franchises, 84
Fund Financial Statements, 271
General Fund Accounting, 284
Goodwill, 79
Governmental Accounting, 254, 255
Governmental Funds, 282, 283
Government-Wide Financial Statements, 261
Gross Profit Method for Estimating Inventory, 54
Hospital Revenues, 312
Impairment, 69
Installment Sales Method, 7
Insurance, 109
Intangibles, 77
Intercompany Bond Holdings, 217
Intercompany Sales of Inventory, 216
Intercompany Sales of Property, Plant, &
  Equipment, 217

Interfund Transactions, 297
Interim Financial Statements, 247
Internal Service Fund, 294
Inventories, 36
Inventory Errors, 38
Inventory Valuation Methods, 40
Investing Activities, 204
Investment Trust Fund, 296
Investments in Derivative Securities, 221
Issuance of Common Stock, 161
Land and Building, 62
Leasehold Improvements, 82
Leases, 116
Life Insurance, 197
Long-Term Construction Contracts, 57, 58
Lower of Cost or Market, 53
Management Discussion & Analysis, 260
Marketable Securities, 194
Methods of Reporting Investments, 187
Miscellaneous Liabilities, 115
Modified Accrual Accounting, 257

Index

Nonmonetary Exchanges, 73, 74, 75, 76
  Exception, *74*
Notes Received for Cash, 91
Notes Received for Goods or Services, 93
Notes to Government Financial Statements, 281
Objectives of Financial Reporting, 1
Operating Activities, 201
Partnership, 235
Partnership Liquidation, 242
Patents, 82
Pension Expense, 146
Pension Plans, 146, 147
Pension Trust Fund, 295
Percentage of Completion, 57
Periodic Versus Perpetual, 39
Permanent & Temporary Differences, 154
Personal Financial Statements, 251
Postretirement Benefits, 150
Preferred Stock, 165
Preferred Stock – Special Issuances, 169
Presentation of EPS Information, 186

Prior Period Adjustments, 172
Private Purpose Trust Fund, 296
Property, Plant, & Equipment, 61
Proprietary Funds, 294
Qualitative Characteristics of Accounting
  Information, 2
Quasi Reorganizations, 178
Refinancing Liabilities, 115
Reportable Segments, 233
Reporting Comprehensive Income, 29
Reporting Discontinued Operations, 28
Reporting Earnings Per Share, 182
Reporting the Results of Operations, 16
Research and Development, 83
Retained Earnings, 171
Retiring a Partner, 240
Revenue Recognition, 7
Royalties, 110
Sale-Leaseback Transactions, 128
Sales-Type & Direct-Financing Leases, 124
Segment Reporting, 232

Service Contract, 111
Software, 84
Solid Waste Landfill Operations, 300
Special Disclosures, 14
Special Revenue Fund, 292
Startup Costs, 84
Statement of Activities, 265
Statement of Activities for NPO, 304
Statement of Cash Flows, 198, 200
Statement of Cash Flows for NPO, 306
Statement of Financial Position, 302

Statement of Functional Expenses, 306
Statement of Net Assets, 263
Statement of Retained Earnings, 173
Stock Appreciation Rights, 177
Stock Options Plans, 174
Stockholders' Equity, 161
Treasury Stock, 163
Troubled Debt Restructuring, 142
Use of Derivatives, 223, 224
Warranties, 113